AROUND THE
CORNER
TO
AROUND THE
WORLD

AROUND THE CORNER
TO
AROUND THE WORLD

A Dozen Lessons I Learned Running Dunkin' Donuts

ROBERT M. ROSENBERG,

Thirty-Five-Year CEO of Dunkin' Donuts

HARPERCOLLINS
LEADERSHIP

AN IMPRINT OF HARPERCOLLINS

Published by HarperCollins Leadership,
an imprint of HarperCollins Focus LLC.

Book design by Pauline Neuwirth, Neuwirth & Associates.

ISBN 978-1-4002-2049-6 (eBook)
ISBN 978-1-4002-2048-9 (HC)

Library of Congress Control Number: 2020941483

Printed in the United States of America
20 21 22 23 LSC 10 9 8 7 6 5 4 3 2 1

Contents

INTRODUCTION

Every morning, six million people around the world start their day with a cup of Dunkin' Donuts coffee. Thirsty customers in search of their favorite pick-me-up can find their fix in more than thirteen thousand stores and in more than forty countries. In the United States, the brand enjoys a 95 percent recognition rate among consumers. In 2008, head-to-head taste comparisons between Dunkin's original brew and Starbucks blend, Dunkin' was preferred 58 percent to 42 percent.[1] In part due to these achievements, Wall Street has placed a market value of nearly $6.5 billion on the enterprise known as Dunkin' Brands (as of January 2020).[2]

This was not always the case. From humble beginnings—a single shop in Quincy, Massachusetts, in 1950—Dunkin' Donuts grew over the years into one of the world's most beloved brands through sheer perseverance and grit, talent, and a little bit of luck. This memoir chronicles the trials and tribulations, the dizzying highs when we got it right and the heart-thumping near-death lows of when *I* got it wrong.

This is a story of a family business transforming from a small, regional diversified food service company into the worldwide, iconic brand it is today. More than anything else, it is a story of change. Sometimes it was a pivotal switch-up in management that affected all levels of the business, or merely a refinement in the menu that sent sales skyrocketing. Deceptively simple adjustments in the service delivery system transformed our retail concept in fundamental ways. A more sophisticated location and marketing strategy increased sales dramatically, while a new purchasing system saved our franchisees tens of millions of dollars. The fact is that our team—both franchise owners and management together—continually adapted to an ever-changing consumer and competitive landscape. This adaptability enabled us to build this world-renowned brand that I had the good fortune to shepherd for more than thirty-five years.

It is my hope that this book will appeal to the millions of Dunkin' Donuts consumers around the world as well as small-business owners, franchisees, and business leaders. Customers will enjoy a peek behind the curtain to learn the stories of how our delicious donuts, coffee, and other favorites like Munchkins®, muffins, and frozen beverages came to be.

Since my time and exposure with this company parallels the mind-blowing growth of the fast-food business, as well as the franchise system of distribution, business readers are sure to find value in this tale as well.

Growing any business is not for the faint of heart; not in 1950 when Dunkin' began, not during the years I was at the helm, 1963–98, and certainly not today. So to all those entrepreneurs building their own businesses today or contemplating buying a franchise, I would hope our successes and failures would be a valuable springboard and provide important lessons and helpful insights—or cautionary tales—for your own ventures.

Finally, I have written this memoir as an ode to the thousands of executives, staff, and franchise owners past and present who have built this wonderful business. It was their adaptability, courage, and genius that made Dunkin' Donuts a legendary and dominant global brand.

This book is organized into six distinct eras spanning my thirty-five years at the helm, each revealing our unique response to the swiftly morphing conditions around us. Every chapter starts with an overview of events, followed by reflections on those events through four lenses. The first is *strategy*. Strategy is the controlling plan that sets out what an enterprise wishes to be, what it wishes to achieve, and the most important action steps it needs to take to marshal scarce resources in the achievement of its mission and objectives. The second lens is *organization*, which deals with the recruitment, retention, and motivation of the appropriate staff to achieve the strategy. The third is *communication*, the aim of which is to align all constituents enthusiastically behind the achievement of the strategy. The fourth and final category I call *crisis management*, where I parse the issues that posed either a threat or opportunity to the enterprise, requiring the attention of the CEO. In my experience, these are the four critical functions of an effective CEO.

Each chapter wraps with a lessons-learned section. Unfortunately, not all of these were learned when they could have been most useful. But after due reflection on three-and-a-half decades at the helm of a dynamically growing business, six years teaching as an adjunct in the graduate program of a leading entrepreneurial college, and decades as a board member of several well-known food service companies, I've become convinced of the worth of this counsel.

ERA 1: 1963–68

HALCYON DAYS

BACKGROUND

On a beautiful sunny June day in 1963, I had a conversation with my father, William Rosenberg, that would change the trajectory of my life. At the time, I was a newly minted MBA, just twenty-five years old, barely two weeks postgraduation from Harvard Business School. On that life-changing day, my forty-seven-year-old father asked me to become president of his business, Universal Food Systems, a daunting responsibility for more reasons than you might guess.

He sat me down in his office, slipping immediately into full sales mode. "Look," he said, "I've observed you over the years, and whether it be school, camp, or the army, you've always come out on top—a leader—and I'm sure you can do this as well."

Wonderful words to hear from my dad; still, I took a huge breath and asked for some time to think.

UNIVERSAL FOOD SYSTEMS

Universal Food Systems comprised a portfolio of eight small food service divisions[1] with annual revenues of $6 million and earnings of $93,000. Up until that point in my life, the only thing I had managed were a couple of donut shops—replacing managers for their summer vacations—and a short stint supervising a cafeteria. My father's request was breathtaking and anxiety-producing, but not all that surprising. A few months previous, while still in business school, I had accompanied him to a meeting in New York City where he was trying to sell the business to a small private equity investor for $1.5 million. He quickly passed on our offer. I had the distinct impression that this prospective New York buyer was only one of many who had already passed on the deal.

My father's one goal—the sale of the enterprise that would become Dunkin' Donuts—was to be a millionaire after taxes.

An eighth-grade dropout and product of the depression, my father had seen his father lose his small market in Boston to bankruptcy during the depression of the 1930s. These are trials I had not gone through, so I could only imagine how they must have scarred him as well as shaped every decision he made. I loved and respected my dad. I had sought his approval and approbation throughout my life.

From my earliest recollections, he had shared his business experiences with me. I vividly recall the day in 1947—I was just nine years old—when he took me on my first airplane ride. It was a DC3 and we flew to Albany, New York, from Boston. His company was providing the industrial catering for the thousands of employees at the Watervliet Arsenal in Watervliet, New York. It seemed the employees were up in arms over the fact that he had raised the price of a cup of coffee from a nickel to a dime. My dad's mission was to try to explain his reasoning and calm them down in hopes of saving his largest and most important account.

I remember sitting in the rear of the union hall with hundreds of grumbling workers as my dad took the stage. A normal man would be a bit addled in this situation, but not my dad. He was fearless. He held forth for the better part of an hour as he explained that the price of coffee had escalated, and he believed they were better served by raising the price rather than reducing the quality. At the conclusion of the meeting, a vote was taken and a majority of the attendees were swayed, now in support of quality over price. That commitment to quality was, I believe, baked into the DNA of every business he started and lives on in the products Dunkin' Donuts and Baskin-Robbins serve to this very day.

My father was a self-made man with an eighth-grade education. Well-built and handsome, he stood a good six feet and weighed in at a solid 220 pounds. The kind of guy who walked into a room and dominated it; someone impossible to ignore. He was bigger than life. And he had the knack—an entrepreneurial zeal that defined and drove him. He was a world-class salesman who could sell sand on the beach. But the more I observed him, the more I came to know that his strengths were tempered by weaknesses.

On the plus side, his timing was great. Returning servicemen and -women entering the workforce after World War II would put a tailwind in the food-away-from-home industry, which grew at a healthy clip for the next fifty years.

My dad also proved to be quite adaptable. When his initial industrial food service business began to falter because of changing competitive conditions, he searched and experimented with other business formats to keep his dream of business success alive. Unfortunately, he didn't know when to stop diversifying.

He had also fallen prey to some of the common mistakes many self-made people make, suffering from an almost unfillable need for recognition. This weakness was exacerbated not only by his upbringing, but—plain and simple—by his personality. His worldview was formed by what I came to understand as a "scarcity mentality." He saw life as: I win, you lose—or, just as starkly—you win, I lose. Nothing in between. If he didn't feel himself the winner, he was utterly miserable. There was no model on earth for him to see life as a win-win for all parties. Even worse, he believed he was infallible, that his success in one area or activity made him an expert and invincible in all others. Worst of all was his habit of taking every last dram of credit for what worked out well while syndicating the blame to others for what didn't. This was his modus operandi.

But after laboring for fifteen years with his business, my father was weary and wanted out. His oft-repeated refrain was that he started supporting his family when he was a boy and had already worked a lifetime. All the males in his family had died young, so he saw hard work as a sure road to an early death. Conversely, he viewed free time as fun and life-extending, so I knew he had that in mind when he made his offer to me.

At that time, in 1957, my parents had begun to spend their winters in Florida. The rest of the year, when my father did come to work in Boston, he had the habit of working out mornings at a downtown health club, arriving at the office by noon, then keeping his staff at work quite late into the evening. He had already turned over the day-to-day management of Universal Food Systems to a former Montgomery Ward[2] executive, S. Joseph Loscocco.

Even before that fateful day when my father turned to me to take over day-to-day management, profits had stalled and he was stymied. He had grown his business from an industrial catering company with trucks serving factory workers—a business he knew well—to a highly diversified portfolio of food service businesses. Profits began to stagnate—averaging between $96,000 and $200,000 yearly. Larger food service competitors, like Canteen Corporation, were winning vending and cafeteria accounts in our region from his Industrial Cafeteria and Menu Mat Vending division.

Our small chain of fifteen hamburger stores, Howdy Beef n' Burger, was suffering at the hands of McDonald's. Our pancake houses had maxed out at just three—Providence, Rhode Island, Coral Gables, Florida, and Burlington, Vermont. Willie's, our New York-style deli in Providence, turned out to be a major cash burner. And the crown jewel of Universal Food Systems—Dunkin' Donuts? Yes, our hundred-store, mostly franchised, chain was in extremis as well.

Exacerbating the problem, Dunkin' management began to lose faith that a limited menu, based solely on coffee and donuts, was sufficient to profitably support a store, so they tinkered with the format and offerings. The last twenty-six stores they had opened varied in size from eighteen to ninety-six seats and served full breakfasts as well as an assortment of grilled foods, such as hot dogs and hamburgers. The operation was complicated and store profits suffered. Franchisees were complaining and failing. Many wanted to spend their 2 percent advertising contractual commitment on their own stores in their own region rather than contribute to the general advertising fund—a potentially ruinous decision.

The ad fund was the essential resource allocated to building our brand and keeping the franchise healthy and expanding. Siphoning off those monies was, in effect, giving up control of where, when, and how the brand would be communicated to the consumer. Despite knowing better, management was beginning to accede to these franchisee requests.

A FAMILY SPLIT

I think the most galling reason my healthy forty-seven-year-old father turned to me to take the reins of his business was the publicity and recognition his former partner and brother-in-law, Harry Winokur, had been garnering as founder of my father's major competitor, Mister Donut. For my dad, this was the most frustrating and damaging set of events imaginable.

To truly understand how corrosive this crisis was for my father and his stalled business, I have to go back to the founding and early history of our company. Our original business, Industrial Luncheon Service, was founded in 1946 after my father had broken up with two partners in Bridgeport, Connecticut. The partnership lasted but six months.

My father returned to Boston, and with a few thousand dollars, opened an exact clone of the Bridgeport operation—same two-toned blue trucks, same name, same menu, and identical method of operation. Out of a small storefront on the corner of Quincy Street and Columbia Road in Dorchester, my uncles, mother, and I rehabbed a commissary. My father, great salesman that he was, nailed the accounts, while my uncles ran the route trucks and served coffee, donuts, and sandwiches to office, construction, and factory workers at local businesses. My mother made sandwiches while I, at nine years old, washed out the coffee urns after school.

As the business grew, my father approached his brother-in-law, Harry Winokur, to become his partner. Harry was a CPA and my father admired his judgment, business know-how, honesty, and way with people. At the time, my father considered Harry his mentor and advisor.

Harry turned his accounting practice over to his partner, invested $2,500, and became a full partner with my father in 1948. The business, then known as Industrial Luncheon Services, grew rapidly; by 1950, a hundred and fifty route trucks were servicing customers from six depots around New England. But the business began to falter as vending machines appeared on the scene, making lunch truck stops outside of a business less convenient.

The head baker in the commissary in Quincy told my father and uncle that the nearby donut shop—for which he had once worked—was making more money from their one retail store than from all twelve of their trucks delivering wholesale donuts throughout the Boston area. As my dad and uncle's own business was being weighed down by the rising costs of truck distribution, the overhead from a commissary, and many far-flung truck depots, they realized a retail donut shop might be just the business diversification they needed.

They rented, for $75 a month, a closed awning shop on the Southern Artery in Quincy, a road connecting Boston and Cape Cod. They opened a donut and coffee shop called Open Kettle in 1948. Disappointingly, the results for this little donut shop were no different from the other fifteen hundred or so donut shops that operated throughout the state at that time: a modest sales take of $1,500 per week—clearly not the panacea they had hoped for.

The Open Kettle had been in operation just a few months when it was rumored a nearby food service operator planned to add a competitive donut shop to his lot. The competitor was Maury Pearl, a former band leader who had made his musical mark with a hit song titled "The Sheik of Araby." My father and uncle moved quickly to head Maury off at the pass—they hired his intended architect, Bernard Healy.

It was Healy who took one look at the windowless stucco shop and declared, "I have to tell you guys: this design isn't doing your operation any favors." According to Healy, consumers were looking for something that would "knock their socks off"—a new California-style fishbowl building where consumers could see what was going on inside. For initial layout ideas, my dad turned to Providence, Rhode Island, equipment supplier Dave Friedman and his firm, Paramount Restaurant Supply. Dave designed a question mark–shaped counter that accommodated twenty stools. This layout served, for better or worse, as our service delivery system for the next thirty years. In addition, Healy remarked that the name "Open Kettle" simply didn't signify what was being offered to the consumer.

So, my dad, Healy, and Friedman had a brainstorming session. Healy asked, "What do you do with a donut?" He soon volunteered, "You pluck a chicken and you dunk a donut." My father said, "*That's it!*"

•

He soon volunteered, "You pluck a chicken and you dunk a donut." My father said, "*That's it!*"

•

The finer points of dunking a donut were made famous by a noted comedian of the era, Red Skelton. Red was well known for creating a comedic skit demonstrating the etiquette and proper technique for dunking a donut in a cup of coffee. Soon after the skit aired, on Memorial Day weekend in 1950, a newly constructed Dunkin' Donuts[3] store opened on the Southern Artery that stopped Maury in his tracks. It generated not $1,500 per week but a whopping $5,000 per week, with coffee selling for a dime and donuts at fifty-five cents per dozen. Same location, same menu, same pricing, same management running the store; but a testimony to the importance of both presentation and serendipity—a revitalized store design. This novel donut-based skit by a wildly popular comedian transformed a middling me-too operation to a retail success and the foundation of an empire.

The success of the Quincy location spawned four additional openings around Boston over the next few years. But the success of the donut shops was overshadowed by a growing rift between the brother-in-law partners, who owned the business fifty-fifty.

It was 1951. I clearly recall nearly every family dinner at that time dominated by my father railing to us about his partner. He claimed that my aunt Etta, Harry's wife, was jealous of the fame and publicity my father was garnering. According to him, she felt my uncle Harry wasn't getting his due. *Coronet* magazine and the *Saturday Evening Post* had published stories about the "meals on wheels" operation, and my father's up-from-the-bootstraps history figured prominently. But letters I have from Harry to my dad suggest his real concern was not public recognition but rather lack of inclusion on important business decisions and meetings; no mention was made about the occasional company write-ups.

My father increasingly saw Harry less and less as a well-educated mentor who added value to the enterprise and more and more as an unimaginative bean counter, a dull weight around his neck. He claimed Harry was holding him back from great success. In his letters, Harry would request that my father refrain from berating him in front of other members of the management team when Harry was not present. He asked that my father not make unilateral decisions but include him. The breakdown became so severe that the partners actually came to blows: my dad took a poke at Harry. Their fights were so frequent, loud, and disruptive that the two men eventually decided to move out of their offices in the commissary in Quincy to separate offices at 25 Huntington Avenue in downtown Boston.

At this point, Harry communicated to my father in the form of handwritten, certified letters sent from his personal residence rather than from his nearby office. Not surprisingly, they both retained lawyers and started negotiations as how to best dissolve the partnership; this continued for months. Just when they were about to throw the matter into court and ask a judge to decide the equities, they reached an agreement in which either party could exercise the option to buy the other out for the 1955 book value of the business, at the time $350,000.

I'll never forget the moment my father was about to go to his attorney's office to make his election. I was seventeen, a senior in high school preparing to enroll at the School for Hotel and Restaurant Administration at Michigan State.[4]

I vividly remember that fateful day my dad had to decide if he would sell his 50 percent of the business to Harry or if he would buy it. It was Wednesday, May 18, 1955. The sun was shining brightly. It was one of those gorgeous midspring days that lifted your soul. My dad paced the living room as he tried to make up his mind.

Buying was the most natural choice for him. His ego and life were tied to his business, but buying meant having to borrow a lot of money. In fact, he'd have to put a second mortgage on our suburban home. It was a sobering moment for him, a child of the depression who had witnessed his own father fail in his Norfolk Street Market, unable to support the debt to finance it.

I strongly preferred for him to buy. Clearly, I was not an uninvolved, independent observer. But I also had a strong sense for what I thought was right for my father. He was still a young man at thirty-eight, and his identity was tied to his business. I reasoned he would be miserable if he were separated from the thing he had worked so hard to create.

I had yet to leave the house to drive to high school and was the last person to speak to him before his drive downtown. I shot my cuffs and went into hard selling mode. It seems the acorn doesn't fall far from the tree. As he prepared to leave, I could tell he was still uncertain. But he had a half-hour car ride to his lawyer's office to make up his mind.

Here's what I said:

"Look, Dad, I strongly urge you to buy! This business has been your crowning achievement. You would be heartsick if you turned it over to somebody else. You said yourself we could get time on the loans from the Hood Milk and the coffee company. I'm sure that if we had trouble our suppliers would give us more time! They don't want to be in the industrial catering business. And, once you're free from Harry, you could franchise the donut shops—a plan you've always said he held you back from."

He was noncommittal when he left the house. In the end, I have no idea what impact my speech had on him. But I know that my dad was always heavily influenced by the comments of the last person to talk to him. I only know that I left for school that day and later, at dinner, learned that he had bought rather than sold. I was delighted.

I also know he was confident that Harry didn't want to be saddled with the industrial catering and vending businesses and would probably elect to sell. So that's the way it went down. On May 18, 1955, my dad agreed to pay Harry $350,000 for his half of the business: a large chunk in cash at the closing and the rest in annual installments. To accomplish this, he had to take out a second mortgage on our home and borrow money from many of the suppliers to our business. It was what happened over the next several years that took its toll on my father.

So what did Harry do? He took the money and started a competitive chain called Mister Donut.

The donut wars had begun.

•

So what did Harry do? He took the money and started a competitive chain called Mister Donut.
The donut wars had begun.

•

THE DONUT WARS

My father maintained that Harry held back some of the best prospective donut shop locations, knowing that the partnership was about to split. George Rittenberg, a Boston real estate lawyer and key location scout, went with Harry and quickly secured four of the best locations around Boston, opening some very high-volume shops in Revere, Medford, North Weymouth, and Westwood. Harry was soon nominated for and eventually awarded the prestigious Horatio Alger Award for his incredible rise from humble beginnings to successful fast-food entrepreneur, much to my father's misery.

The first book ever written on franchising was *The Franchise Boom* by Harry Kursh, published by Prentice-Hall in 1962. The book was the sole and most important chronicle of this new and explosively growing business system called franchising.

The Franchise Boom opens with the Harry Winokur story and features it throughout. William Rosenberg is mentioned just once— and briefly—on page 150, and only as one of many who helped form the International Franchise Association. Mister Donut was prominently featured on a popular television program, which awarded a free franchise to a couple before a national audience. It created a lot of buzz.

All of these developments called into question who the real driving force was behind the donut business at the time. To complicate matters, my mother, father, aunt, and uncle all traveled in the same social circle. All were privy to my father's tales of Harry's timidity and, in comparison, his own superior accomplishments. But it seemed Joe Loscocco and company were impotent in the face of this daunting competition. Numbers didn't lie. Burdened by a difficult set of other portfolio businesses, it was starting to look like Dunkin' was about to be overtaken by Mister Donut. It was an excruciatingly painful time for my dad.

It was against this backdrop—a tangled knot of familial, financial, and logistical pitfalls—that I was being asked to assume responsibility and turn the ship around.

A BIG DECISION

The decision as to whether to assume responsibility for the company weighed heavily on me. In the six weeks leading up to that decision, I had been working alongside Loscocco, the executive vice president, familiarizing myself with the business and finding a position within the organization where I could fit and add value. In the process, I became familiar with the members of the management team and how they spent their time. My biggest lesson here was that, although there was a wide range in talent, the senior team was reasonably competent at their operational duties.

Head of donut operations was Jack Delahunt, a former University of Massachusetts basketball player and former Howard Johnson's junior executive. Jack was cousin of and bore a strong family resemblance to former Massachusetts congressman Bill Delahunt. Jack had an eye for talent and a good way with people.

Among Jack's team was a very talented regional manager, Ralph Gabellieri, who started in Providence as a donut baker and then store manager. At the time, in early 1963, the stores in Rhode Island had been suffering unsustainably low sales. When Ralph became regional supervisor, he developed and executed a strategy of delivering donuts at wholesale to cafeterias in local factories. In his determination to succeed, Ralph would drive from outlet to outlet—knocking on doors and windows—handing out the donuts and taking in the cash. Single-handedly, Ralph brought all the stores to profitability and, in the process, became a legend throughout the company.

Sam Bader was a World War II veteran. Although he never spoke of it, Sam's face bore the scars of a terrible explosion. Sam previously worked at Endicott Johnson Shoe Company as an expert in real estate and later at Rayco, a well-known 1950s franchise chain that specialized in recovering auto convertible tops and seat covers. Sam was brought in to provide franchising and real estate experience. Quiet and tough, Sam was a Hungarian refugee who grew up on the streets of New York City. It was Sam, based on his previous franchise experience, who continually whispered in my ear to convert our franchise agreements from a rebate to a royalty. This proved to be a life-or-death issue for our business: had we not changed, we would have been litigated out of existence. He didn't talk a lot, but when he did, his comments were worth hearing.

Norman Slater was a comptroller, CPA, master bridge player, and an attorney by training. Although generally the most abrasive of the group, he was by far, in my opinion, the most brilliant team member. He had a keen eye for trends and new marketing innovations. It was Norman who established our first West Coast regional office, and from his beat in California saw and reported on the benefits of a hot dog concept called Der Wienerschnitzel and their pioneering drive-through window service delivery system. This was in 1967, a full decade before it became a fast-food standard. I attribute our being an early adopter of drive-throughs to Norman's advocacy. In the end, he did not want to be a comptroller. He longed for a line job, not a staff job. His personal objective was to make some good money and leave the company to become a college professor, which is exactly what he did.

Jack Alpert was the family and corporate lawyer. Although a sole practitioner and not an employee, Jack worked as an advisor, involved in many of the day-to-day activities of the company.

The weakest member of the team, as I saw it, was our head of marketing. He was more of an executor of other people's ideas rather than someone who contributed his own. I thought he lacked the imagination and creativity to head what should have primarily been considered a marketing company.

This team spent the majority of their time huddled in Loscocco's office, Joe puffing endlessly on his pipe as they debated how to put out the daily fires—most of which had to do with store closings. Attention was drained away on tactics, not strategy. There was never a coherent conversation concerning strategy or any discussion at all about creating guidelines to help handle these recurring issues.

During my second year in business school, I was fortunate to take courses in retailing taught by the acknowledged dean of retailing, Walter Salmon. I also studied strategy at that time under Seymour Tilles, one of the founders of the Boston Consulting Group. Tilles's course provided the framework and language I needed to understand the process of strategy creation. The course in retailing gave me the opportunity to write required papers about the strategic issues facing Universal Food Systems. Both courses created a wonderful confluence of learning and real-world demands. Much to my disappointment, however, none of the issues explored in depth in my classroom were talked about or even touched upon in Loscocco's smoke-filled room. Loscocco's training had come from his experience at a large and soon-to-be-outmoded catalogue and department store chain, Montgomery Ward. As the days and weeks wore on, I was quickly coming to the conclusion that the problem with our company lay with leadership.

The only counsel I took in deciding whether to take my father's offer was from my wife, Lorna. She encouraged me to take the job and was sure I would become successful. If I had a concern about the downside, it was if I were to fail, *would I be employable?* I thought it more than possible that a future employer might not want a twenty-five-year old failed CEO. Wouldn't they worry that I might consider an entry-level job beneath me? And what would my choices be after that? I shuddered to think about it.

During those first few weeks, my father checked back with me to see how I was faring in coming to a decision. To try and seal the deal and have me finally assume responsibility for the business, he told me, "Look, you get Mother and me a million and a half dollars, and the business is yours." I never had him put this in writing; in fact, as the value of the business escalated, I didn't think it fair to do so, and—had he done so—never would have held him to it. He later denied ever saying it.

Money had never been a consideration as to whether I took this job. My decision was based solely on my assessment of whether I could do the job better than Loscocco. When I was in college, and later, while a student in business school, I had worked summers relieving managers in both cafeterias and donut shops during their summer vacations. In exchange, I received $40 a week throughout the year and had the use of a company automobile. Out of the $2,000-a-year salary, I was responsible for my living expenses and tuition. I was married before I entered business school, and my wife, Lorna, worked as well. Although her salary helped defray our expenses, by the time I graduated, I had to borrow an additional $16,000 from the company to make ends meet. Even so, an increase in compensation was the furthest thing from my mind. I never negotiated repayment of my debt or salary with my father.

On July 15, 1963, eight weeks after graduation, I reached my final decision. I told my dad I'd take the job, and I became CEO of Universal Food Systems. My salary that first year was $15,600. My father informed the senior management team of his decision to put me in charge, and as you might expect, they were in shocked disbelief.

"Are you crazy? He's only twenty-five years old!" was the collective response. Others said, "What will Loscocco think? What will he do?"

I have two recollections from that day. The first is a phone call from Jack Delahunt saying, "Kid, you'll be okay and I stand behind you." The other was a conversation I had with Joe Loscocco himself. I confess, I was quite nervous but just as quickly calmed down when I saw that he seemed to be taking it all in stride. I told him I'd appreciated all that he had done to steward the company over the last several years, but I couldn't have an executive vice president between me and my management team. I gave him a choice. I offered to have him stay as administrative vice president without specifying the exact remit of his duties, or he could leave the company with severance. I suggested he take a couple of weeks off to think about it and get back to me.

I have no idea from where the intuition came for me to decide early on to eliminate the buffer between me and my management team. Perhaps it came from a class in business school. As I look back, my repositioning of his role was essential if I were to lead that organization. In the end, Loscocco decided to leave. During that stressful time, I couldn't help thinking that part of what makes a true leader is the fact that he or she has followers. I was fortunate that the others stayed. If the other executives decided to follow suit, I could have been known for having the shortest tenure of any CEO in commercial history.

And so, I began. My desk wasn't actually a desk—it was the far end of a long conference table resting on the uneven floors of the second story of The Regent, a 1926 movie theater at 440 Hancock Street in North Quincy. Not only was this table the sole conference table in the company at the time, but I had to share it with every large group meeting the company held.

My father no longer had a need for his personal assistant and secretary, Lee Schultz. But she proved to be indispensable to me. In the early days, her knowledge about the company proved invaluable, and for twenty-seven years she loyally helped me through countless ups and downs, days both disastrous and promising. At that moment, crises were flying at me left and right, all day long. Still, I faced the future with equal measures of trepidation, anticipation, excitement, and hope.

HITTING THE GROUND RUNNING

The first few days of my presidency in that summer of 1963 were a blur. During my first week on the job, two of our franchised Dunkin' Donut shops in northern New Jersey closed their doors forever. The news was a real downer around the office. These shops had enjoyed initial success, and their failure raised questions about the viability of the donut and coffee concept as a stand-alone business, its expansion to locations outside of New England, and ultimately the job security of those who earned their living from the business.

In that same first week, the franchise owner at our New Bedford location made an appointment with me. I was dumbfounded when he handed over the keys to his newly opened food-donut shop; I simply had no idea as to what to do or say. I excused myself, left my office. As luck would have it, I bumped into Sam Bader in the hall, who suggested I try to convince this disgruntled franchisee to give the store a little more time before throwing in the towel. I did, and luckily he agreed. In time, we converted the store to a straight donut shop, and it exists to this day as one of the higher-volume shops in the system.

During those early days, I was besieged with unpaid bills from contractors who slapped liens on the stores under construction for extras they claimed were due them. There were neither written documentation on change orders nor procedures as to how to handle them. I spent every Saturday, from early morning to late at night, sorting through their claims and settling them on the phone, one by one getting the liens lifted. Most often, the franchisees who sublet the locations from the company already had their rents fixed on the basis of preliminary costs; therefore the company was forced to "eat the extras." It was a condition I hadn't expected, and I was intent on finding a solution—quick.

Having given me his "office" in the conference room, my father had no place to sit at 440 Hancock Street, so he rarely made an appearance at headquarters. But he would call frequently to rail about Mister Donut's progress and check on what I was doing to turn the tide and perceptions. In 1963, the Dunkin' Donuts store count stood at one hundred, and the Mister Donut count was eighty. I had little success convincing my father that the American public could care less about who was the first and biggest donut shop chain—they just wanted the best, most convenient product at the best price.

But I have to admit, I was caught up in the competition as well. Within a few months of my assuming the presidency of Universal Food Systems, my uncle Harry promoted his son-in-law, David Slater, to CEO of Mister Donut. Three years my senior at twenty-eight, he had also been my junior counselor at summer camp when I was a kid. As a result, my father knew him well and respected him.

The donut wars had now officially advanced to a second generation and promised to be just as intense as the famed conflict between the Hatfields and the McCoys.[5]

●

The donut wars had now officially advanced to a second generation and promised to be just as intense as the famed conflict between the Hatfields and the McCoys.

●

STRATEGY

Despite all the emergencies flying in daily over the transom, I did find time in those early days to meet with my team, and together we began to lay out a new and explicit strategy. Within the first few days, we agreed we would not open any more combination food-donut shops. These were complicated operations, more costly to build and less profitable to operate. In fact, they were undifferentiated from a common diner. On top of that, stores ranged from eighteen to ninety seats, further blurring our image. We agreed on a standard donut and coffee shop, featuring a twenty-seat counter in a question mark configuration. We standardized our menu to feature fifty-two varieties of donuts and a standard six-ounce cup of coffee served in a porcelain cup over the counter, and in a six-ounce to-go paper cup.

This decision was tested early on when Jack Delahunt came into my office. In those early days, we caught an important break. A new store was under construction in South Bend, Indiana. Since we had called for an immediate halt to construction of any additional food-donut shops, all those currently being built had to be converted to our now standard twenty-seat donut shop configuration, including South Bend. On that day, Delahunt explained that the prospective franchisee for South Bend had contracted for a food-donut shop and was insisting on that configuration. I asked him to offer the franchise owner his money back and said we would open the store as a company-owned location. The franchisee took his money back and—holding our breath—we went ahead with our twenty-seat store.

In an era where the average volume for our one hundred locations was around $2,200 per week, South Bend came roaring out of the gate at $9,000 per week, and we made a $9,000 profit as a company-owned store in the first month of operation. A store that promised to make $100,000 in annual profits was a big deal to a company that had earned just $200,000 from its entire operation in its best year. Needless to say, the senior management team breathed a huge sigh of relief, as did I.

We also made the difficult decision not to sell franchises in every market where we had an interested franchise buyer. We decided to restrict our expansion to specific markets designated for growth, where we could eventually afford supervision and advertise our brand.

We also agreed that we would deny any prospective franchise owners the option to change their agreements, specifically to spend their advertising money for their own stores. Rather, we agreed to build our advertising fund and launch a comprehensive campaign that would showcase our brand.

The benefit from that strategic decision quickly became evident when a second fortunate break came our way. I received a call from the marketing head of Mister Donut, Carl Zucker, who told me he was not getting along with David Slater and was looking to make a change. He asked if I was interested in talking. I certainly was, and soon. Shortly thereafter, Carl came to work for us and replaced our existing head of marketing.

Two things occurred in a matter of weeks. Mister Donut was no longer making huge public relations coups, possibly because Carl had left. More importantly, Carl quickly convinced me that adding a second coffee to-go size of ten ounces to complement our six-ounce cup would be a boon to business. Carl quickly designed a ten-ounce cup and created a new name for it. Our launch of Jumbo Java, our first new product, marked the first time we had some real news to advertise to our customers. Same-store sales (comparison of store sales this year to the same period the previous year) skyrocketed by over 12 percent during my first twelve months on the job. This same-store sales gain was *better than twice as much growth as any in our history*. This first campaign enabled us to prove dramatically to our franchise owners the unquestionable benefits of combining our ad dollars in mass media campaigns rather than squandering it in local newspapers.

New-store growth was an additional strategic initiative. In the early days, most franchisees lacked sufficient credit and the brand strength to warrant landlords leasing directly to them. As a result, the company found it necessary to sign the lease and in turn sublet the location to the franchisee at a markup against a percentage of sales, whichever was the greater. Since most leases were a twenty-year commitment and represented how we were to distribute our brand, I felt it necessary to visit each new location before signing a lease or purchasing the land.

We were committing to an entirely new strategy. No additional pancake houses would be opened—neither would any other new business venture be launched. There would be no more food donut shops. It was Dunkin' Donuts—the newly defined Dunkin' Do-nuts—and nothing else. This was a declaration that would prove to shape all of our actions in fundamental ways. We were betting the ranch on just two prosaic products: a cup of coffee and a donut; not unlike the empires built on tomato ketchup, a chocolate bar, or some caramel-colored carbonated beverage in a bottle. We were putting a stake in the ground. We were committing to be the best in the world at delivering the world's most delicious coffee and donuts. As this new strategy began to unfold, there were some very promising signs. I was beginning to cement a following among senior management as well as franchisees. And most importantly, it all felt right to me, and I was falling in love with my job.

•

No additional pancake houses would be opened—neither would any other new business venture be launched. There would be no more food donut shops. It was Dunkin' Donuts— the newly defined Dunkin' Donuts—and nothing else.

•

THE STORY BEHIND DUNKIN' COFFEE

The delightful and stimulating effects of coffee were discovered about five hundred years ago in Yemen. It took about a hundred and fifty years for the product to make its way from the Arabian Peninsula to Europe, then in the next century to the rest of the world.

Coffee is one of, if not the most complicated and labor-intensive crops to get from farm to cup while maintaining quality. It starts as a berry from the Coffea plant. This five-layer cherry-like fruit is grown in high, mountainous regions by thousands of small farmers in seventy equatorial countries around the world. First, the cherries are picked and dried, then the seed kernel (often called the bean) is separated from the fleshy part of the berry. This very laborious process is often done by hand.

Brazil grows about one-third of the now $70 billion coffee market. Brazilian beans are brought to the port of Santos where they are painstakingly graded—manually—according to size and imperfections. These grades are denoted as Santos two through eight; two being the highest quality and eight the lowest. Beans are shipped to roasters around the world who then blend and roast the coffee.

From its inception, Dunkin' strove to offer the most delicious cup available anywhere. We started with a blend of the best Arabica beans from crops originally grown in the Arabian Peninsula, as opposed to Robusta beans, which originated in sub-Saharan Africa. Our blend was composed of the highest quality Brazilian coffees combined with Colombian and Central American Milds: beans grown in the mountains of Guatemala, Honduras, and Nicaragua.

Since coffee is an agricultural product, dramatically affected by climactic conditions from year to year, adjustments in formula must be made from shipment to shipment to meet our end-product specifications. We sought a full-bodied coffee, mildly roasted, with a clean, sparkling finish.

We selected the best roasters from around the country, for the most part small firms that had consistently demonstrated exquisite taste and skill in delivering coffees that met our standards. To ensure freshness, we distributed our coffee to our stores weekly, in bean form only. Once the beans arrived, we'd grind them to order in small batches in full view of the customer. We found the Bunn Coffee Machine was the best to brew coffee in small batches. We brewed no more than sixty ounces at a time. The rule was that brewed coffee never sat around for more than eighteen minutes from the time it was brewed until it was served. During the brewing process, we made sure the coffee steeped at no more than two hundred degrees, since coffee degrades if allowed to boil. In addition, our coffee weight to water was significantly higher than any of our competitors. For example, Tim Hortons, a competitor from Canada, used pre-ground coffee and their ground weight per sixty-ounce pot was 25 percent less than ours. More ground coffee with the same amount of water per pot made for a more full-flavored, less bitter cup of coffee.

Since our commitment to quality culminated with the final beverage served, we were as fastidious about the cream we used as our brewing process. Dairies distinguish milk products by the degree of butterfat content. Heavy whipping cream, at 40 percent butterfat, is the richest, while half and half is 10–12 percent butterfat, all the way down to milk that may contain no butterfat at all.

We believed our coffee tasted and colored best with 18 percent light cream. The problem was, very few dairies had enough customers who used this custom cream to make it worth their while to produce it. In our opinion, there was nothing like the mouth feel and flavor that a fresh, light cream brings to a cup of coffee. Our job was to find and convince local dairies in each market to make the cream for us. It was no easy task.

THE STORY BEHIND OUR DONUTS

The existence of fried dough products stretches back nearly eight thousand years to the invention of pottery, which enabled ground grain products to be fried in oil. Their popularity surged in the sixteenth century when the Dutch made oliekoek (oil cookies) to celebrate the Yule time. That tradition was carried to the New World when the Dutch founded New York. Myth has it that the product was transformed when, in 1847, a Maine sea captain, Hansen Gregory, accidently punched a hole in the fried dough to create the ring-shaped treat we now know as a donut. The product grew in popularity in America when the ladies of the Salvation Army served our World War I soldiers donuts as a treat; rumor has it that this is one of the reasons our soldiers were called "dough boys."

In the twentieth century, the Leavitt family in New York helped popularize donuts by manufacturing donut mixes and donut machines. Their company was called Donut Corporation of America (DCA). They also opened a small chain of restaurants in New York City called The Mayflower Donut Shoppes. I vividly remember the motto on the wall of their shops: "As you go through life, brother, always make this your goal, 'keep your eye upon the doughnut and not upon the hole.'"

The Leavitts also invented a small frying machine called the Robot Turner, which automatically dispensed the raw dough product into a canal of frying oil, automatically flipping it at the right time. A customer could enjoy a hot donut on the spot. These Robot donut machines were a big hit at fairs, carnivals, and festivals.

If delivering a quality cup of coffee requires the most labor-intensive care from crop to cup in the beverage category, the same could be said about delivering high-quality hand-cut donuts in the bakery category. We lavished the same kind of attention and love on the quality of our donuts as we did on our coffee.

There were four types of donut mixes we used to make the infinite varieties we sold. The first, and by far the most popular, were the donuts leavened by yeast. Yeast donuts were the base for all the honey-dipped rings we sold, as well as the shells, which contained all the yummy real fruit fillings, from jelly (which in our case was a combination of apple and raspberry fruit) to blueberry and lemon.

Yeast-leavened donuts were particularly challenging and time-consuming to produce. The process began with the mixing. In order to ensure the yeast was released properly, exact dough temperatures were crucial.

The yeast donuts were made in twenty-five to fifty-pound batches. They were mixed for twenty minutes, allowed twenty minutes to rise, then separated into loaves on a large hardwood table covered in canvas. The loaves were allowed to rest another few minutes before cutting. With the help of a little dusting flour to prevent the dough from sticking to either the rolling pin or the canvas, each loaf would be rolled out flat, then "shrunk" to relax the dough. Bakers used a round cutter to cut ring donuts, careful to cut close so as not to leave too much scrap. These rings were either honey dipped or frosted, and were known as "first cuts," the most tender, since the dough was not yet reworked with minimal dusting flour to toughen it.

To see a skilled donut baker cut a loaf of rings was a sight to behold. He'd cut with one hand, and as the ring donuts popped up, impale them on the fingers of his other hand to be laid on a screen for proofing and ultimately frying.

The scrap would be rolled and loafed yet again, the loafed dough allowed to rest for a few minutes before being rolled out and cut into shells. Shells are the round donuts, looking like fluffy little pillows, filled with all those amazing real fruits or Bavarian Krème fillings. These shells are known in the trade as "second cuts." Loafing would take place yet again. Then these "third cuts" would be used for coffee rolls or tarts, or as we called them, "fancies."

The next step in the process was equally critical. All yeast donuts are allowed to "proof" before frying. Proofing is the process where temperature and humidity are controlled to allow the dough to rise before frying. Since atmospheric conditions are always changing, this step required a skilled baker to adjust the humidity and temperature in the "proof box" to ensure the product was neither over- nor under-proofed.

Finally, the donuts were neatly placed on their screens, ready for frying, an equally challenging process. The three-foot mesh screens were lowered in pure vegetable shortening at 375 degrees, until the donuts floated free of the screen. After one minute of frying, the baker would use a pair of chopsticks to quickly turn the donut to its other side—careful not to stick the chopstick into the donut, allowing shortening to rush in and ruin the end product.

Finally, the product was ready for finishing. The rings were placed, hot out of the fryolator, on long sticks to be rolled into a large mixing bowl of honey dip, or to cool a bit before being frosted. The shells were allowed to cool, then filled by hand pumps with three-quarters of an ounce of filling.

A yeast mix donut could—from start to finish—take four hours, while a cake mix yielding plain cake rings and crullers took half an hour. While the plain and chocolate cake mixes didn't need the same fermentation and proofing time, a great deal of care and skill was needed to create a stellar treat.

Cake donuts used softer wheat (less gluten than the hard wheat used in yeast donuts). Baking soda replaced yeast for the leavening process. Dough temperatures were equally critical. In the early years, we were so concerned with keeping the cake dough tender that we mixed only by hand rather than in the large Hobart mixers used for yeast products. A dash of nutmeg was added to plain cake mixes in our New England shops, just vanilla for the rest of the country. Cake donuts fry up with a delightful crunchy exterior and a tender, cakey center.

Rounding out the basic mixes was a French cruller mix. French crullers are basically a fried popover, meaning they have a high egg content. The mix was fed into a special machine that sat over the fryolator. The baker would crank out the spiral-shaped donuts, which were either honey dipped or frosted, and out-of-this-world good.

By this point I think you've got a sense of the physicality and skill it took to make high-quality donuts. If a customer had the patience and time to watch an eight-hour production shift, I suspect it might have looked like an intricate and deftly choreographed dance: the dance of the donuts.

ORGANIZATION

The senior management team began to consider another idea I'd had in graduate school. Since we were now going to restrict growth to specific, media-defined marketing areas around the country, we thought it might make more sense to decentralize the organization. Our thinking was that rather than have all the talent at headquarters at 440 Hancock Street, we could keep the New England Zone there but also open an office in metro New York City for stores in the Mid-Atlantic region, Chicago for the Midwest markets, and an office in the West for stores in that region as well. Each office would be headed by a vice president responsible for real estate acquisition, franchising, and ongoing operations, while the staff functions of marketing, finance, legal, and human resources would remain centralized at headquarters. Our belief was that we could not only grow faster but enjoy stronger ongoing operational support by keeping our senior people closer to the action.

Norman Slater, our CFO, had longed for a line job and was the first to volunteer to pioneer this organizational format. Norman opened our western region office in Portland, Oregon. Sam Bader agreed to move back to New Jersey and open an office in Teaneck to oversee growth in the Mid-Atlantic States. In New England, Jack Delahunt manned operations. For Chicago and the Midwest, I hired Sylvan Spira, an old franchising hand. For decades, Sylvan had been part of the senior management team at Tastee Freez, which was headquartered in Chicago.

To replace Norman as CFO, I tried to hire Bill Beebe, one of my classmates at business school. As married students, Bill and I would drive back and forth to school together from our off-campus apartments each day. We became great friends. Bill was at Goldman Sachs in New York City where he worked in their corporate finance department, a job he had taken after graduation. It seemed impossible to lure him away to the less glamorous world of a donut and coffee company in Quincy, Massachusetts. So I turned to my cousin Leonard Swartz.

Nine months my senior, Lenny was a CPA for Arthur Young in Boston. On weekends when we were twelve or thirteen years old, our job was to climb into and clean the fifty-gallon coffee makers at our main commissary for the industrial catering company. As a teenager, I worked successive summers first in the central kitchen, then the bakery, while Lenny served as the porter for the first Dunkin' store on the Southern Artery in Quincy. In 1964, Lenny joined the company as CFO. He played the key role in securing financing with Commercial Investment Trust for our prefabricated building program. A year later, when I was finally able to convince Beebe to leave Goldman and take the CFO job, Lenny moved to Teaneck to assume operational responsibility for the Mid-Atlantic stores, while Sam Bader took on real estate and franchising.

Sam Bader had strongly suggested I meet a young entrepreneur named Frank Tumminello. At twenty-seven, Frank had already built and sold over forty-five coffee and muffin shops in greater New York City, all walk-in locations. Frank's modus operandi was to build a store, operate it for six months, then sell it for a capital gain. Because of the recurring nature of these transactions, Frank's lawyers told him the government would likely disallow this favorable capital gain tax treatment in the future, which was one reason I think Frank was open to talk employment with Dunkin'. Also, up to that point, we had never opened an urban location.

Frank joined the company and taught us his methodology for in-city location selection, working with other vice presidents to open high-volume city locations around the country. This enhanced our ability to penetrate markets as well as build distribution and brand awareness. When Sylvan Spira didn't work out in Chicago, Frank moved his family there and assumed operational responsibility for the Midwest region. Frank's stay with the company was only about three years, but we have remained close friends. He was a constant source of ideas, suggestions, and insights as to changes in the industry and their implications for Dunkin' Donuts.

Carl Zucker possessed an entrepreneurial gene to match his marketing one, and he petitioned me to support his decision to move to Houston and buy the franchise rights for the entire state of Texas. We had no stores in Texas and no plans for any. I acceded to his request, and as a result I hired Irv Eisen, a former ad executive and senior marketing executive for Pine-Sol as a replacement for Zucker as head of marketing.

One of my major organizational dilemmas at the time was the lack of procedures in our building process, which was the reason for my Saturday soirees spent sorting through extra bills and negotiating settlements by phone with contractors. One obvious solution to this problem was to replace Al Christoffers who headed up construction. Christoffers came from a background of building metal porta-ble diners, and he would constantly pitch me about what a boon to our development program such a prefab building would be.

Donut shop buildings could be financed in one of four ways. The first was for the company to buy and mortgage the land, then build according to our specs. This method required a lot of cash, and with our weak balance sheet, we could only build a few new stores a year. The second was to either have the landlord mortgage his land or find an investor to buy it and then mortgage the land to build the building. This was called a "build to suit" and was the primary way in which we grew. The third alternative was to lease a piece of land and ask the landlord to "subordinate" his interest to allow us to use his land to obtain a mortgage and build the building. Rarely if ever was a landlord willing to subordinate his land for someone else's building. The fourth and final way was to take a straight land lease from a third-party landlord and build the building with company cash. Again, this was very capital intensive, and therefore a real growth inhibitor.

A prefabricated building was one notion where we could obtain land leases and—if we were skillful enough—convince a finance com-pany to treat the building as something portable, like equipment, so we could obtain financing. This would allow us to move faster and—because it didn't require the landlord to mortgage his property—would allow us to lease the best locations in a community. The promise of faster and better growth prompted me to help finance Christoffers's plan to start a prefab building program in a factory he located in Elizabeth, New Jersey. He called his venture Trans Steel. His vision was to build small, portable buildings for restaurant chains such as Dunkin' Donuts. We agreed to buy his first round of produc-tion. I also quickly replaced him as head of design and architecture with a trained and licensed architect, who developed processes that straightened out the extras and liens. These new procedures finally took me off the rack and freed my Saturdays to be in the field looking at new locations and existing operations.

Another important job opening came in 1965 when our head of human resources resigned to run for governor of Massachusetts. I turned to Bill Beebe, by then CFO, and asked if he could recommend a replacement. That was when I learned about Tom Schwarz. Bill said Tom was one of the smartest people he knew. Currently in the corporate finance department at Goldman Sachs, Tom expressed a lot of interest, going so far as to say he might be open to the idea of working not just on transitory deals but on building a company over time. His concern with the Goldman job—and its attendant time-pressured environment—was that it would rob him of the chance to properly parent his growing family of three children.

My conversations with Tom went on for a few months. I liked him immediately and neither of us was put off by the notion that he had no prior human resources experience. But it took a bit of selling to get Tom to leave the renowned banking firm of Goldman in New York City to head up personnel development for a relatively unknown company in Boston. Eventually, Tom came around, and he and his wife, Ann, and family moved to Boston at the beginning of 1966.

Finally, I felt I had an organizational format and the personnel in place to execute the strategy we as senior managers had agreed upon. We had four regional offices: Boston; northern New Jersey; Chicago; and Portland, Oregon. Regional vice presidents could now focus on building the brand in the few key cities in their purview. Our operation was especially strong at headquarters: with Beebe in charge of finance, Schwarz at personnel, and Eisen heading up marketing, I felt our future was exceedingly bright and promising.

COMMUNICATION

Early on in my days as CEO, we ran some ads with varying success. We really began to build a campaign and brand recognition when Irv Eisen came on board. Irv switched the Boston agency that had handled our account to a New York firm called Daniel and Charles. Their entire team grilled Irv and me on the nature of our business and the important issues we faced. They quickly came to understand that we were concerned with developing consistent product quality and high operating standards throughout the system.

In restaurants, there are basically six meal "occasions" through-out the day: breakfast, morning coffee break, lunch, afternoon snack break, dinner, and late night. In the early '60s, lunch and dinner accounted for more than 70 percent of sales away from home, snacks about 12 percent, breakfast approximately 8 percent, and off hours 10 percent. Since Dunkin' Donuts competed as an eat-in option during the breakfast and snack and evening periods only, we had to rely on the sale of donuts for take home to achieve sufficient sales volume to make our concept work. This plan was in stark contrast with concepts like McDonald's, which had offerings in 100 percent of the meal occasions.

To ensure freshness at that time, ideally all the donuts were made throughout the day. Generally speaking, product purchased for take home at night—one of the heavy donut-buying periods—would be consumed the next morning for breakfast. Our standards called for all our baked goods to be sold no more than four hours from production, ideally to be consumed no later than breakfast the next morning. The heaviest production period for donuts was the night shift, which ran from 11:00 p.m. to 7:00 a.m.—which made sense.

A good donut maker could cut and finish three hundred dozen donuts in an eight-hour shift. As you might imagine, these donut makers were a prized and essential part of the shop operations. I fondly remember a visit from Ellie Leary, one of our opening crew personnel, when I was running a few shops in Hartford, Connecticut, after hotel school. She told me a story that sticks with me to this day and underscores how precious these donut makers were. Norman Revard, a legendary donut maker, was not a feast for the eyes—on the unkempt side, never clean shaven, with only one tooth and maybe a hundred pounds soaking wet—but when that man showed up for his production shift at eleven in the evening on the dot, Ellie would say that, to her, Norman Revard looked just like Cary Grant. If he didn't show up, and there were times when these guys simply didn't, it was up to the store manager—Ellie—to stay up all night doing his job, quite often staying right through the day for her shift as well. There were quite a number of times I had to pick up the slack.

But it was the second shift that had become the quality problem. This was the afternoon shift, generally manned by the franchise owner or store manager. I had found that there was little or no donut production in that shift—since the staff tended to rely on the evening production to carry the shop throughout the day. Consequently, baked goods turned stale—clearly a violation of our four-hour rule—and sales during the evening were slipping. To solve that, the decision was made to cut back from three hundred to two hundred dozen donuts during night production, while making one hundred dozen in the afternoon to ensure freshness and try to build back our evening business.

To support this change, Daniel and Charles developed our first television advertising campaign in 1965 called "The Pledge," featuring actual franchise owners from all over the country. They appeared in this iconic thirty-second spot dressed in their white uniforms and high toque hats holding a cake donut in their right hand as they pledged to make donuts fresh every four hours, coffee fresh every eighteen minutes, and that their "cream would never be milk." The production values of the commercial were superb. We spent a total of $250,000 on the campaign, but it was effective in changing store behavior, raising freshness standards and sales in the process. This fondly remembered commercial resonated for years with franchise owners and consumers alike.

To achieve franchise owner support, Irv and I traveled all over the United States meeting with franchise owners in small groups in local hotels, sharing our findings, and urging them to correct the production and quality deficiencies. We also used this opportunity to share our values and vision for the business. It was an excellent opportunity to hear their side of things and develop personal relationships.

The ability to spend time with both our franchise owners and members of our field staff underscored for me the benefits of face-to-face time. I also gained an understanding of the energy and persistence it takes to sell in a strategy or new processes. Remember, these were the days before FaceTime and linked-in live conferences. Training videos and newsletters were sometimes necessary but much less useful.

CRISIS MANAGEMENT

During those early years, there were several critical decisions I was called upon to make. To some, I responded wisely and—I think—correctly. In others, I made the wrong call. Hindsight is certainly 20/20, perhaps especially in the world of business.

The most crucial determination had to be how we made our money as a franchisor. When the business was launched, we profited by making a rebate from suppliers on all the goods that were purchased by franchisees. Therefore, we made a rebate on flour, shortening, coffee, cream, uniforms, and so on. At the time, there was concern among lawyers who followed franchising that these arrangements might be a violation of the law.

The Sherman Antitrust Act passed at the beginning of the twentieth century held that it was a per se violation in restraint of trade to require the purchase of one item if it was tied to another. Basically, you could not force the franchisee to purchase any goods unless you could prove the goods were unique. The remedy under law for the guilty party was treble damages. This was a huge sword of Damocles hanging over our system, threatening its very existence. Loscocco and company were aware of this risk and moved to restrict rebates to just five items they felt could be argued were unique. For all other items they deemed fungible, such as cream and uniforms, they negotiated a fixed monthly payment in exchange for allowing franchise owners to negotiate directly with their suppliers on those products. Problem was, there was no rhyme or reason to the amounts negotiated. The monthly charges bore no resemblance to quantity or to any standard as far as I could see but rather depended upon the negotiating skill of the parties, generally ranging from $20 to $100 per month.

Sam Bader, who had experience with this threat in his previous jobs, kept urging me to scrap the whole system and move to a straight royalty, which was unquestionably legal. He argued convincingly that the tied products were not unique. Franchisees could buy comparable donut flour and shortening on the open market at lower prices, since they had no rebate included. Proponents of the tie would point to the Carvel case where the courts held Carvel could require franchisees to buy soft ice cream mix from the company because the product and the brand were inextricably tied. I was chastened by what I saw as the botched fixed-dollar agreements signed just a year or two before my stewardship, but I was encouraged by the story Keith Roper told at the International Franchise Meeting in 1964 in Lake Arrowhead, California. He was a senior manager of United Rent-All, and he related how he had shifted his two hundred franchisees from a rebate arrangement to a percentage of sales royalty.

It was just the right message at the right time. Like Rent-All, we had about two hundred stores at the time. I returned to headquarters and asked my cousin, who was CFO at the time, to calculate our rebate percentage. It was 5.2 percent. I decided we'd open our books, show each franchise owner how much we were a making in rebates, and ask them to sign a royalty arrangement of 4.5 percent. We would agree never to make a rebate again. It was a huge risk. It was possible one or several franchise owners would take the information to an attorney and sue for restraint of trade and treble damages in a class action law suit.

That would have spelled the end of Dunkin' Donuts.

•

That would have spelled the end of Dunkin' Donuts.

•

Much to my relief, all but one of our franchise owners agreed to the new terms. As it turned out, those franchise companies that did not move to a royalty system but continued to make their money on rebates were eventually sued and subsequently failed. The change in contract turned out to be my first, but not my last, near-death experience as a CEO.

Another decision I was called upon to make in those early years had to do with the sale of the company. My father continued to put pressure on me to explore selling the company. The better the yearly results, the greater the pressure. He would regale me with stories about people he had met on the golf course who would tell him they were once worth $10 million but lost it all because events and time had turned against them. "Shame on them," he would say.

Pressure ramped up as a rash of restaurant companies began selling out to large food manufacturers. In the 1960s, most consumer goods companies were awakening to the fact that a huge shift was afoot in the way food was being sold. Nearly 50 percent of food was purchased away from home and away from supermarkets, its traditional source of distribution. As a result, Pillsbury bought Burger King for $18 million from Jim McLamore, General Foods scooped up Burger Chef from Frank Thomas, and General Mills purchased Red Lobster from Bill Darden. Pepsi first gobbled up Pizza Hut from the Carney brothers, then they bought Taco Bell from Glenn Bell. Quaker Oats launched Magic Pan, their own restaurant chain. We didn't escape the attention of these food manufacturers either.

At the suggestion of one of our donut mix suppliers and my father's urging, I found myself—along with my dad—with Nate Cummings, owner of Sara Lee (Consolidated Foods) at the Waldorf Towers. Ensconced in Nate's beautiful dining room, replete with Impressionist masterpieces, we enjoyed a lavish breakfast as we listened to what was a tentative and unsolicited offer of $7.5 million for Dunkin'. I asked for some time to think it over. I was opposed to the idea of selling, and I was even more strongly opposed to listening to offers.

This whole issue came to a head in June of 1967. My entire family—my sister, Carol; my brother, Donald; my mother, nicknamed Bookie; my father; me; and my wife, Lorna—were attending my brother's graduation from prep school. After the ceremony, we all gathered in a booth at a Howard Johnson restaurant near Cheshire, Connecticut. It was there my dad made his case for selling the business.

He pointed out that a lot of smart operators we knew well had decided to sell, insisting that the time was right for us to do the same. He repeated his stories about golf course buddies who were once worth $10 million but now that the tide had turned didn't have a thin dime.

This was not a new conversation for me; in fact, it was one we'd had countless times over the past few years, and each time it caused me great anxiety. In the booth that day I made the same point I always had, that when running a business, all hands had to be on deck. That it was impossible to run a business successfully with one foot out the door and one still kicking the competition to the curb, which included our nemesis, Mister Donut. Further, I argued, our recent record had been stellar, and if that trend persisted we could go public and the money would come. Truthfully, however, at that point, most of the stock in the company was owned by my father, and the rest of the people around the table didn't stand to make much.

Dad, as was his habit, pressed the point, contending, *if not now, when?* This was one of the most intellectually challenging moments I had to face in my early years. My answer certainly wasn't to be found in books or graduate school classes.

After a few moments spent gathering my thoughts, I proposed what I believed was an original notion. The time to sell is not when an offer comes over the transom but rather when you have neither the energy nor the ideas to achieve your financial objectives. That is the time to sell and allow another management team, one that *does* have the vison and energy, to pick up the baton. Still, no matter how much I believed in what I was saying, I had a very large lump in my throat. Yes, we were growing at an incredible clip, and I had a lot of faith in the future of the company. But just then, sitting with my clan over lunch, I was turning down a substantial payout not only to my dad but to my entire family.

It was a decision I never regretted. Nate Cummings and Consolidated Foods went on to purchase Chicken Delight. Unfortunately, Chicken Delight was one of those companies that made its money from rebates on supplies sold to their franchisees, a practice deemed illegal. Unable to pay treble damages, the company went out of business. Conversely, I watched the value of our enterprise go from an unmet asking price of $1.5 million in 1963, to a public offering price of $40 million in 1968, to a value of $320 million in 1990, and finally to a public value of approximately $6.5 billion (as of January 2020).

On the negative side, a decision I did come to regret was our early entry into England in the fall of '64. I had gotten a call from my dad to clue me in that Mister Donut was about to go on a trade mission to England and Germany for the express purpose of opening the European market. "Surely, Bob, we can't allow them to do that! We risk losing a four-hundred-million-person market to our archrivals and contenders for the crown of the most important donut company in the world." It all sounded right to me.

So off he went with a small entourage on a state department tour. He held press conferences and made big news in the *Financial Times* and elsewhere announcing how we were going to open stores in England and Germany and teach Europeans all about franchising.

Upon his return, he suggested I rehire Loscocco to represent us. Loscocco had worked as a consultant after leaving Universal Food Systems and advised Pillsbury, a Dunkin' supplier, on their Burger King acquisition, but he had yet to find permanent employment and was willing to relocate to London to head our new European operations. What a deal! Off my father went back to Florida or to his health retreat in Durham, North Carolina. Off to London went Loscocco and up went my expense charges for a Hyde Park office, a secretary, and a chauffeur for Loscocco.

Unfortunately, there was little progress to show for all this international expense. On my first trip to London in 1965, Loscocco took me to a failing supermarket on Edgware Road near Hyde Park corner. I later discovered the supermarket owner had become Loscocco's personal chauffeur after the supermarket failed. A year later, we did open our first location in Ludgate Circus near Fleet Street, not far from Saint Paul's. Sales were poor, as Londoners had yet to gain the habit of coffee to go in paper cups and breakfast away from home. We were primarily seen as a bakery with little eat-in or to-go business.

Our second location was on High Street in Ealing, a London suburb, and had equally tepid results. I asked Frank Tumminello, our in-city specialist, to give his assessment. After two years and hundreds of thousands of dollars in expenses, Tumminello advised me to give it up. The London market had proven just too different an eating-away-from-home culture, and our resources and management were insufficient to change it. I agreed and after two difficult and costly years, closed the whole operation down. Mister Donut, perhaps reading the same tea leaves, never opened a store in Europe after all.

GETTING READY TO GO PUBLIC

Another activity that required my personal attention was getting the company ready for a public offering. The strategies we put in place and the organization we created to execute those strategies had worked extremely well over that five-year time period. Store count had risen from 100 to 267, while average volume per store had grown from $111,000 per year to more than $140,000. Corporate profits had exploded from $133,000 at the end of 1963 to $727,000 (eighty-seven cents per share) at the close of our fiscal year in 1967, amounting to an eye-popping 50 percent compound rate of growth.

A public offering was the only strategy to fend off a sale of the whole company and monetize my father's holdings, a commitment made to my dad years earlier. To enable the best sendoff, we took several strategic steps to put in place a number of key elements.

To assure the public that our financial statements were reliable, we used the services of a then Big Eight public accounting firm, Price Waterhouse, as our accountants. The noted Boston law firm Ropes & Gray guided us on any stock issues, their association implying we were handling our prospectus and representations correctly. A few years previous, my father had established an executive stock option program with the help of Ropes & Gray, setting aside 10 percent of the company's common stock for options for key executives.

We banked with the Bank of Boston, the same firm that McDonald's used. Bill Brown, our account manager and eventual CEO of Bank of Boston, advised us on how to best present our creditworthiness by arranging a $1.5 million loan from John Hancock Insurance Company. Paine Webber was selected as our lead underwriter to manage the initial offering; the same company that led McDonald's initial public offering in April 1965.

To broaden our board of directors, we added several outside members. Joining my father and me on the board were Richard W. "Archie" Southgate, partner and eventual managing partner of Ropes & Gray; Milton Brown, Lincoln Filene Professor of Retailing at Harvard Business School; and Homer Severne, retired senior vice president of finance at John Hancock Insurance Company, our lender.

BENEFITS OF AN EXPANDED BOARD

It didn't take long to feel the benefits of having some outsiders on the board. Milt Brown quickly championed the notion of tightening our focus even further. He argued that although we had reduced allocation of cash resources and time behind our industrial catering, vending, and hamburger businesses, maybe we should consider exiting those businesses entirely. His arguments proved compelling and we proceeded to do just that.

Bill Beebe put a process in place to sell the vending and cafeteria business, ultimately negotiating a $1 million sale to one of our largest competitors, Canteen Corporation. We reached accord with the twenty Howdy Beef n' Burger franchise owners to allow them to keep the name and certainly their locations, but we were going to cease being a franchisor of that brand. Many of those franchise owners also owned or shared sites with Dunkin' Donuts stores. They continued under the Howdy brand, while other franchise owners rebadged their restaurant to other food brands. These last acts put an official end to Universal Food Systems. We were no longer a portfolio of many disparate food businesses but a streamlined and focused donut and coffee company.

The stock market at the end of the 1960s was incredibly robust. Though the country was simultaneously waging and funding a war in Vietnam as well as a war on poverty at home, the burdening effects of the Johnson administration's guns and butter policies had yet to affect the stock market. In fact, the effects of those policies were not to be felt by the stock market until the early 1970s.

THE BIG DAY ARRIVES

On February 6, 1968, the renamed Universal Food Systems, underwritten by PaineWebber, went public as Dunkin' Donuts Incorporated with an offering price of $20 per share. We were the third fast-food company to go public following McDonald's and Kentucky Fried Chicken.

The first trades came in quite strong and the stock price soared that first day. The market had finally picked up on the mind-blowing growth potential in the away-from-home food industry; demand for the stock was feverish. At February's close, the bid was $32.75, up 60 percent in three weeks. My father sold 229,000 of the 300,000 shares offered that day, retaining a 45 percent ownership of the business after the offering. After broker commissions, he netted almost $4.5 million in cash proceeds; that money plus the remaining shares he owned easily made him the millionaire he always wanted to be. He moved eighty miles away to Exeter, New Hampshire, where he became an instant gentleman farmer with the purchase of a several-hundred-acre farm where he bred and raced harness horses.

The company also sold about fifty thousand shares that day, amounting to just over a million dollars, adding handsomely to the company's coffers.

The entire management team as well as my family members, who either had options or were gifted stock, were jubilant.[6]

In retrospect, it looked as if we were being rewarded with the same accord and multiples that defined, in future years, the dot-com era. Before long, Dunkin's stock was trading close to a breathtaking $66 a share. What a turnaround! A company that couldn't fetch $1.5 million in 1962 was now worth more than $120 million. What more could I have asked for as I approached my thirtieth birthday?

THE END OF THE DONUT WARS

Another of the achievements of that era was the successful conclusion of the donut wars. It was rumored that Mister Donut had expanded in far too many markets, which resulted in both low store sales and multiple closings, decimating corporate profitability. David Slater left the employ of my uncle Harry to start a business of his own, and the company lost momentum. Uncle Harry and Slater decided to follow the path of other fast-food pioneers of the times—get out of the business. Uncle Harry eventually sold Mister Donut for $6 million to their flour supplier, another Minneapolis miller, International Multifoods.

LESSON ONE:
Leadership Is Paramount

The most important lesson I learned over these years is the paramount role leadership plays in the success of any entity. Be it the United States government, a company, or even a family unit, influence flows from the top down. If the leadership shows itself incompetent or of poor character, it cannot be fixed from the middle or the bottom. It can only be remedied with a replacement at the top.

In my experience, successful leadership is part art and part science. The portion that is art—qualities like empathy, creativity, aspiration, and introspection—may be instinctual, traits that someone may be gifted at birth. The science component deals with the science of management that focuses on concepts, practices, and skills. I think both can be taught, possibly the science more readily than the art. In my opinion, one doesn't have to be a naturally born leader to be successful.

The best lessons are handed down from able mentors, individuals who have manifested practices and philosophies that have resulted in demonstrably effective leadership. My business school professors were my first inspiration, but as time went on, I was galvanized, educated, and coached by a mix of seminars, books, and my fellow colleagues. In retrospect, it becomes clear that a healthy dose of humility can be the best asset in the pursuit of learning and betterment.

A word to would-be entrepreneurs who aspire to a leadership role in their company: apprenticeship plays a major role in the likelihood of success. This became crystal clear to me shortly after I retired and began teaching franchising as an adjunct professor in the graduate school at Babson College.

Offering the pinnacle of entrepreneurial education, much of Babson's program offerings stemmed from the work of Jeffry Timmons and subsequently from his collaborator, Babson professor William Bygrave. For his doctoral thesis at Harvard Business School in the 1960s, Timmons investigated what actions or inactions affected the odds for entrepreneurial success.

Timmons's research illustrated that 80 percent of successful entrepreneurs launch their business in an industry where they have worked at least three to five years. My father's launch of Industrial Luncheon Service supports this finding. For years he worked to build routes for truck food sales before starting his own business in that field. He understood the language, the metrics for success, and most importantly, knew how to design his business to nail a sustainable competitive advantage—tough nuts to crack if you aren't in the business! He always ran into trouble when he strayed from his path. His forays into other businesses where he lacked this crucial knowledge and experience were simply less successful. Yes, his move to donut shops did work out, but I would contend that any success achieved resulted from skills of subsequent managements.

●

[Eighty] percent of successful entrepreneurs launch their business in an industry where they have worked at least three to five years.

●

The concept of success being greatly enhanced by three to five years of apprenticeship dovetails with Malcolm Gladwell's contention in his 2008 book, *Outliers*. Based on studies of elite performance, Gladwell noted that success was "an extraordinarily consistent [result] in an incredible number of fields . . . you need to have practiced, to have apprenticed, for 10,000 hours before you get good."[7] Five years of forty-hour workweeks adds up to just more than ten thousand hours. Of course, there are serial entrepreneurs, those who launch booming businesses over a range of industries, but the odds for success overwhelmingly favor those who have apprenticed in their industry. One of the biggest reasons franchising is such a successful business model is because it abbreviates those many years of necessary apprenticeship through rigorous training programs that distill decades of experience.

LESSON TWO:
Family Businesses Pose Unique Challenges

Most businesses around the world are family owned and managed. Yet, amazingly, only 30 percent[8] successfully transition to the second generation. Fewer still make it to the third. Often, the reasons stem from family conflict. And, more often, that breakdown arises from changing roles and poor communication.

A flashpoint can occur when leadership passes from the founder to the next generation. As a business goes through these transitions, I believe the contribution of the founder must always be honored. It is an unalterable fact that without their vision and fortitude in starting a business, there would simply be no business. That said, unlike a nonfamily business, it is my observation that most founders never see themselves as fully retired from the business they birthed. As a result, the "retired" founder can become a barrier to the change that must occur if a business is to grow.

For example, as a company scales to one hundred employees, leaders—once plugged into every detail—are now required to possess different skills. They now must manage managers. Changing the old ways can often spark conflict between the founder and the new generation of family leadership. In my case, bedrock adjustments in strategy, organization, franchise contracts—even the name of the company itself—had to change if the enterprise was to flourish.

Issues over remuneration and equity can also lead to conflict in a family business more easily than in a nonfamily enterprise. I have seen companies in which the owner has not been explicit about his or her personal objectives. Some founders see their objective as building an enterprise beyond themselves. They define success if the business flourishes by passing it on to successive generations. Conversely, there are founders who see the business as their creation, and as such, believe they are entitled to harvest the majority of the value from the business in their lifetime.

Another potential complication of a family business can be the differing and sometimes overlapping roles of family members. All are family. Yet some may also be involved in managing the business and some may not. There may well be differing levels of ownership within the family. These differences often prove fertile ground for jealousy and grievances.

For a family member, joining a family business can present a significant opportunity. It can also present some unique challenges. I hope that by identifying some of these concerns, those who are joining family businesses will be aware and undertake conversations to clarify roles and equities. Today, unlike the 1960s, there are many well-qualified consultants specializing in family enterprises who can help families sort out these very knotty issues.

In the 2017 movie *The Founder*, Ray Kroc appropriated undeserved credit for founding McDonald's. The movie made clear that it was not Kroc but the brothers Dick and Mac McDonald who were the geniuses behind developing the service delivery system that revolutionized the restaurant industry.

Still, it was Ray Kroc who saw and exploited its potential. The fact is, it often takes a village to create a lasting enterprise. In the case of McDonald's, the McDonald brothers and Ray Kroc needed one another to succeed. I would contend that the same symbiotic relationship existed for my dad and me. Fortunately, if the business is successful, there should be enough credit and financial reward for all who help create and grow it.

LESSON THREE:
Quality Matters

I am hard pressed to think of any long-lived business that doesn't have, at its core, exceptional quality in either its products or services. This is particularly true in the food business. Whether it's Heinz Ketchup, Budweiser's Beechwood aged beer, or Hershey's chocolate bars, each product shares two common attributes: they're all delicious and they're all created from the finest ingredients. For me, at Dunkin' and Baskin, that meant we used real cream, real fruit, and the finest spices and flavorings we could find.

This belief in the pivotal importance of choice ingredients was instilled in me during a visit to the Watervliet Arsenal when I was nine years old. During a contentious meeting that day, my dad argued passionately for quality over price. This conviction was reinforced early in my presidency when my father told me the story of Charlie Lubin, a man he met during one of his many extended stays at the Rice House Diet Center at Duke University in Durham, North Carolina.

My dad couldn't have been more excited for me to meet this guy, the baker who founded Sara Lee. Charlie's best-known product was the Sara Lee pound cake, which he had popularized in the 1950s, followed by numerous high-quality frozen baked goods sold at supermarkets. So off I went to Chicago to meet Charlie, who by now had sold his company to Nate Cummings of Consolidated Foods—yes, the same Nate Cummings who had offered $7.5 million to buy our company, an offer I had turned down.

Charlie and I met for lunch high up at his dining club that overlooked LaSalle Street in the loop. After a delicious meal and a bit of small talk, I turned to him and asked, "So, Charlie, my dad said you had the answers to success in the food business. What would you advise a young man like myself?"

He took some time, then leaned over the table and in a whisper uttered, "Buttah."

I was taken aback. I said, "Excuse me, can you repeat that?"

He said, "What do you think a pound cake is?"

I responded, "I have no idea."

Charlie then told me something I never forgot: "A pound cake is a pound of flour, a pound of sugar, and a pound of butter. Butter tastes absolutely delicious—there is no substitute for it—it's the real thing."

On my flight back home to Boston, I reflected on my conversation with Charlie. It was clear that any success we had to date had been as a result of our unyielding commitment to product quality, and it was at that moment I vowed that choosing the best ingredients would continue to inform every future product decision.

At that time, we sold only two main products, coffee and donuts. Our quality had to be top notch in order to distinguish ourselves from anything else offered in the marketplace. Dunkin' was the first food service chain to make coffee the centerpiece of its menu. Sure, the occasional fine hotel or restaurant went to great lengths to serve a superlative cup of coffee, but these were the exception to the rule.

In 1950, the coffee business was beginning what would become a fifty-year decline in coffee usage, yet we were growing despite this mighty headwind. Poor quality, vacuum-packed, and instant coffees, along with the growth of other caffeinated beverages like colas, were cutting the average per capita consumption of coffee bought from forty-five gallons per year in 1946 to less than twenty gallons by the year 2000.

To combat that trend, we committed to offering the best cup of coffee in the world. We were unyielding in our pursuit of quality. We even went so far as to have twenty-seven pages of specifications on how to prepare and serve this wonderful brew.

Our devotion to donuts was as focused and painstaking as the attention we lavished on our coffee. I contend that it was our uncompromising pursuit of quality from our inception in the early 1950s that propelled the donut to become one of America's all-time favorite treats.

In my thirty-five years with the company, I cannot recall even one conversation that suggested altering quality to save on costs. Just the opposite. As an example, when ultra-pasteurized 18 percent butterfat cream became available, it offered lower cost due to its 180-day shelf life.[9] Nonetheless, it was quickly rejected because we thought it just didn't taste as good as the standard pasteurized cream. Our attitude about quality can best be summed up by a joke that circulated around our office: "White bread is rye bread that underwent a profit improvement program."

Our quest for quality didn't end at our ingredients. We were just as serious about teaching franchise owners and store staff the intricacies of producing consistently stellar products in our shops. Within weeks of becoming CEO—never shy about appropriating a good idea when I saw one—I borrowed an idea inspired by McDonald's University. DDU (Dunkin' Donuts University) was born in September of 1963.

The first four weeks of the six-week training program were spent mastering the creation of the product itself: how to mix the dough, roll and shrink it, proof and fry it. Sounds simple, but it was tricky. The making of donuts was very much an art. As opposed to hamburgers—the creation of which was always the same (McDonald's food products were made elsewhere and delivered to the restaurant for grilling or frying)—our owners had to manufacture and adjust for varying humidity and temperature to create an acceptable product.

Then there were the daily realities of the business: One worked fast in a hot kitchen over a fryolator, often getting splattered with sizzling shortening. It took a lot of hand-eye coordination to get the job done. To pass, a student had to demonstrate the ability to make two hundred dozen donuts, up to spec, in an eight-hour shift. If the student couldn't come up to par, they wouldn't graduate, and we would return their money. Not everyone was cut out for it.

If they passed the "practical" exam, students spent the last two weeks on management, studying best practices relating to marketing, personnel management, and store profitability. Since we had no classroom or any conference space at 440 Hancock Street, the management portion was held at the end of my long conference table. I might be dictating a letter to Lee Schultz, my secretary, while a DDU class of four or six people was in session at the other end. Since I really had no prior experience with standard office procedure, this whole arrangement did not feel awkward or strange to me.

A FALL FROM GRACE

BACKGROUND

The time is April 1974 and the place is the boardroom in our headquarters in the Randolph Industrial Park in Massachusetts. Our quarterly meeting was coming to order. Bob Howard, a friend of my father and new board member, sat across from me. (Howard was the founder of Centronics, a company that made printers for computers.)

Bob cleared his throat, then turned to me. "Bobby, the results these past three years have been disappointing to say the least. In fact, this past year the company had a $1.7 million loss. The stock is trading at less than two dollars a share and the board has decided to make a change. We want you to search for your replacement."

I was taken aback, but somehow collected myself and found my voice. "Searching for my own replacement is inappropriate. That's the board's responsibility." All eyes on me. I felt the sweat bead on my forehead. "Look," I continued. "We understand the problems that have led to this debacle—we've corrected them. The solutions haven't had a chance to pay out yet. I ask you to let me lead for another quarter to see if I'm right about this. Then we can evaluate whether a search is in order."

I took a deep breath, got up, and left the conference room to let the members discuss the situation and decide my fate.

So what went wrong? How could a company that seemed so well positioned in 1968 morph into such an unmitigated disaster five short years later? Not only had we lost $1.7 million, or eighty-two cents per share in 1973, but our profits had fallen off a cliff in the two years previous to our loss in 1973. In 1970, continuing our unbroken string of 30 percent–plus earnings growth, we had earned ninety-five cents per share. But that proved to be our high-water mark. The subsequent year, earnings had fallen precipitously to fifty cents per share and improved to only fifty-five cents by 1972. These results were incredibly disappointing and a far cry from our objectives.

We were also embroiled in a treble damage class action lawsuit instigated by eight of our franchisees. If an antitrust violation and class were decided against us, the potential damages could have skyrocketed to more than $80 million and spelled the end of Dunkin' Donuts. On top of that, we were ensnared in a stockholder class action suit in the first district of New York in connection with a secondary stock offering we had made the year before. Finally, we were in the process of shuttering eighty of our six hundred shops and had assumed operation of another twenty to prevent them from closing. We were teetering on the precipice of unmitigated disaster, the collapse of everything we had worked for.

The responsibility for our problems—every last one of them—was mine.

●

The responsibility for our problems—
every last one of them—was mine.

●

STRATEGY

Upon graduation from business school, I envisioned our future as a focused donut and coffee company. By 1968, I had become less certain and had begun to develop a new vision. I began to think of our company as a franchising company rather than just a retailer of donuts and coffee. My reasoning, faulty as it was, went something like: if we could grow earnings per share at 50 percent–plus per year with a donut and coffee business, as the law of large numbers came into play—the larger the base earnings, the greater the incremental dollars needed to be generated to maintain growth of earnings per share—we stood a good chance to continue that record-breaking pace by franchising other concepts as well. That shift in vision and mission was a significant change that was to cast a huge shadow over all of our activities for the next several years.

What were the dynamics that led me to such a transformational notion? At the time, I was serving as treasurer of the International Franchise Association and would become that association's tenth president in 1970. (I had served as treasurer, then vice president, and finally, chairman.)

The International Franchise Association, or the IFA, was the only trade association that represented the franchise system of distribution. Its mission was to provide educational and lobbying resources for its members, especially the benefits, best practices, and potential pitfalls of this system. The organization comprised several hundred members, including major bottlers such as Pepsi, food service franchisors like McDonald's, and service system franchisors including Manpower, United Rent-All, Snap-on Tools, and ServiceMaster.

Preceding me as chairman of the IFA was Al Lapin, founder of the International House of Pancakes, or IHOP. Al, at forty, was ten years my senior. He was an LA guy, a charismatic leader in the process of forming a diversified company using the franchise model as its key competence. He had already purchased Love's, a chain of West Coast barbecue restaurants; Orange Julius; and Bryant Schools—a chain of secretarial schools. Al had approached me about buying Dunkin' Donuts to add to his franchising empire. I passed on that idea but was intrigued by his vision and his dreams. Maybe franchising was a better business for growth than a donuts and coffee business alone.

That change in thinking was to take the company and the attention of its senior managers in a new direction, one with big implications. I began to focus not on our Dunkin' Donuts business but on new franchising opportunities. I explored several avenues: opening a national chain of men's haberdashery stores with the Hat Corporation of America, and—with IBM—a chain of learning centers to help young people with remedial reading and math skills.

Those initial pursuits never came to fruition, but one idea we pursued to actual operations was a fish and chips chain we named Charles Goodlight Fish and Chips. I had traveled to England often in the 1960s in connection with our abortive effort there, and I was impressed by the number of fish and chips shops throughout the UK.

Meeting Haddon Salt at an IFA meeting influenced me as well. Haddon, a Brit, founded a chain of fish and chips restaurants in the US called—not so strangely—H. Salt Fish and Chips. I had observed over the years that most successful fast-food concepts had their origins in delicious foods that were easily eaten by hand: items like pizza, fried chicken, hamburgers and French fries, tacos, and donuts—and most were too difficult or messy to be prepared at home. So it was not too much of a stretch for us to decide and try our hand at a chain of fish and chips shops. It didn't hurt that Haddon had quickly sold his chain to Kentucky Fried Chicken for a cool $15 million.

I brought on board a friend of Tom Schwarz, George Haggerty, as vice president of development. It was George's job to oversee Charles Goodlight Fish and Chips, as well as to lead our diversification efforts at finding other concepts that could be quickly grown using the franchise system.

If business diversification wasn't distracting enough during those years, I ventured, yet again, into international development. Not sobered enough by my losses in Britain, I sought and sold a master franchise for Japan to the highly successful, diversified, and publicly owned retail group Seibu. This was once again in response to a strategic move made by Mister Donut. Although Mister Donut never expanded into Europe, they did issue a master license for Japan before their sale to International Multifoods in 1968.

Mister Donut's licensee was a privately owned (and very successful) franchise company headquartered in Osaka called Duskin, which had a unique way of conducting business. They franchised territories to individuals who—for a fee—called on households in their district with the intent of swapping clean dust rags for soiled ones. Hence the name Duskin: "Dust King." The company was founded and led by spiritual leader Seiichi Suzuki, an adherent of a religious organization called Soka Gakkai, a Buddhist movement that holds community service as one of its core precepts. Before a franchise was sold for either a Duskin or Mister Donut in Japan, the prospective franchisee had to knock on a stranger's door and offer to clean the bathroom. This exercise was designed to see how committed the prospect was to a life of service to others. This Japanese Mister Donut franchisee was to prove to be a formidable competitor. In the early 1970s, I spent a good deal of personal time—several weeks per year—negotiating our license and launching our operation there.

If changing the *mission* from a focused domestic coffee and donut chain to a franchising company wasn't problematic enough, I also set the wrong *objective* as well. But I was riding high on success. Growing earnings per share by more than 50 percent in the previous five years was heady stuff, and having a stock trading at forty times earnings was beyond intoxicating. It led to my blissfully ignoring the problem attendant to the law of large numbers.[1] One mistake I made was to grow too fast. In those days, my accountants, Price Waterhouse, allowed us to reflect as income the entire up-front franchise fee of $15,000, irrespective of whether the store had opened or not. To book the money, I only needed a signed franchise agreement and to have a designated location.

To further spur growth, Bill Beebe, our CFO, was able to convince our lender, CIT, that there wasn't much difference between our "movable" prefab stores and conventional masonry buildings. In the end, the prefabs proved unworkable because of intractable construction problems. But now the real estate department, armed with the ability to sign land-only leases without worrying about building financing, could grow the chain at an incredible rate. Within five years, we had opened more than two hundred of these leased locations, adding more than $25 million in owned buildings to our balance sheet.

So what was the problem? We were financing prefab buildings over a seven-year amortization schedule—like equipment—rather than the traditional twenty-year life associated with all such long-lived assets. This would be fine if you could handle the mortgage payments; not so fine to be freighted by such heavy debt if times went against you. And, of course, I was tacking on the cost of additional real estate and franchising executives to grow the system in each of our five regional decentralized offices. At our peak, we were opening 140 new stores a year.

My duties, among many others, included maintaining quality control over site selection of these new stores. I'd leave home at dawn every Tuesday and return bleary-eyed Thursday night, criss-crossing the country as I checked out the new locations. My method of madness was this: in each town, I'd tool around the neighborhood of the proposed store and pronounce, with a thumbs-up or -down, whether the location was a go. No metrics other than my own hunches. Somehow, I thought God had imbued me with this sixth sense, an ability to determine if a site was suitable by casually looking around. Time would soon prove I had no such otherworldly gifts.

Contributing to this already extended agenda, I invested in two ill-conceived R&D projects, enlisting Arthur D. Little, a consulting firm in Cambridge, Massachusetts, to help us with both. The first was the development of an automated machine that could crank out donuts, eliminating the need for the increasingly scarce donut maker. The second was to develop a process to deliver high quality frozen pies to be baked in each store, an idea inspired by the success of just a few newly opened Marie Callender's pie shops in California. Both endeavors proved costly and unsuccessful; in 1973—the year we pulled the plug on the donut machine—we suffered a $1.7 million loss; $500,000 from this ill-advised idea.

I learned two valuable lessons from that experience. First, it's wiser to ask an open-ended question of a consultant rather than tasking them to fulfill any prescribed notion. Had I not led the conversation with such specific expectations—a donut-making machine—and instead asked for an alternative production process that wouldn't compromise quality, things might have turned out differently.

I made the same mistake with the pie project. The better request would have been to ask Arthur D. Little for their help to develop a process for selecting complementary new products, rather than telling them to develop a pie program for us.

The second lesson learned was the crucial importance of distinguishing between a fad and a trend. Marie Callender's pie shops proved to be the former, as did H. Salt Fish and Chips. Had I not been so impatient—had I waited a year or so to see how these products panned out in the marketplace—a lot of painful and costly missteps would have been avoided.

Worldwide geopolitical conditions were not helping our cause. The Middle East oil embargo curtailed automobile traffic. The ban on the Sunday sale of gasoline added to our burdens, Sunday being our busiest day. To top it all off, Nixon's price controls would not allow us to pass on commodity cost increases to our customers.

Price Waterhouse changed partners on our account in 1971, adding to my woes. The new partner, Art Segal, challenged our practice of recognizing the whole franchisee fee as income as soon as the franchise was signed and a location secured, a practice that had been sanctioned by the firm for the past fifteen years. Art argued that the fee should not be booked until the location actually opened for business. This was a painful proposition. We had had a secondary stock offering that year, and the company had just sold $2 million in stock. We argued against the proposed change all the way to the managing partner of Price Waterhouse at the time, but to no avail. Income for half of the 140 stores opened that year had already been booked and had to be taken off the books, reducing income dramatically in 1971. Stockholders who purchased shares in that year's secondary offering sued both Price Waterhouse and us in a stockholder class action suit in federal court.

ORGANIZATION

The concept of decentralization was not necessarily a bad one, but I had placed too much pressure for growth on each of the regional vice presidents without giving them the tools necessary to handle such expansion in a quality way. The pressure to open stores led us to veer from our past policy of staying focused on building our brand in specific markets; instead it was pure numbers, pure growth. Quality suffered.

Carl Zucker, our state licensee for the state of Texas and former marketing chief, had expanded rapidly with fifty new stores. What happened with these stores showcased just how blind I had been to not only regional differences but to the impact of opening in a market where well-loved competition—the Lone Star and Shipley donut chains in this case—had been rolling along for decades. Our Texas stores were failing and closing at a fast pace. Zucker couldn't fulfill his development agreement and backed out, leaving us to pick up the pieces. Shops that had opened in isolated markets in the South and Midwest had similar dismal sales and were shutting their doors one by one, a drumbeat of failure that was beginning to sound all too familiar. In 1973, our *annus horribilis*, I was forced to reserve more than $1.5 million to cover the cost of all the closed stores, in addition to other write-offs.

There were other damages, beyond the balance sheet. Bill Beebe, my old business school friend, now CFO, lost confidence in my leadership and resigned from the company. His departure came as a severe loss to me personally—a real blow to a decade-long friendship—and to the company as well. This was a smart and able guy, whose input and guidance I valued highly. He had also led me to Tom Schwarz, now a key player and someone who would play an even bigger role in the company in the months and years ahead. Jack Alpert, our family and corporate lawyer since the early 1950s, died of a heart attack at age fifty-eight. It was among our company's darkest moments—a very sad and tumultuous time.

COMMUNICATION

Unlike earlier years, when I would travel to regional meetings and meet face-to-face with franchise owners, my contact with these crucial players was now limited to my speech at the annual convention. Now my time was taken up flying all over the country assessing new locations, as well as traveling back and forth to Japan to negotiate and launch our operations there and attempt to flatten Mister Donut. And increasingly, I was spending up to a third of my time on International Franchise Association business. I was a very busy guy, with not a lot of downtime or even time for my family. My communication was increasingly being done in Washington as part of my IFA leadership duties and not spent among my staff and franchisees.

The International Franchise Association was formed at a "Start Your Own Business Show" at the Stockyards in Chicago in the spring of 1959, four years before I assumed leadership of Universal Foods System. Many of the exhibitors were newly formed franchise companies looking to find franchisees to grow their burgeoning brands. The exhibitors, dissatisfied with the quality of the show, decided to throw in $10 apiece to start a trade association that would not only run more effective shows, but also work to educate practitioners, the public, and legislators about the benefits of the franchise system of distribution. They rightly reasoned that no company could undertake that role on their own.

My dad was among the attendees that morning when they raised $1,900 and named themselves what—at the time—seemed a presumptuous title, The International Franchise Association. They elected Al Tunick, founder of Chicken Delight, as its first president. He served in that role for the first two years while Elmer Winters, founder of Manpower, served as the first vice president.

How prescient these early pioneers proved to be. Franchised brands like Burger King, Holiday Inn, and H&R Block were immensely successful and were popping up all over America. Accompanying all that success, however, were some growing abuses.

By the late 1960s, the franchise method of distribution had come under severe scrutiny. Legislation was being proposed in Washington and various states that would have severely crippled the viability of the franchise system. As the remarkable success stories of McDonald's, Kentucky Fried Chicken, and Dunkin' Donuts spread, promoters began to conclude that a well-known name associated with a product was the recipe for a multimillion-dollar public offering. So almost overnight, Jerry Lewis Movie Theaters, Minnie Pearl's Chicken Houses, Conway Twitty's Twitty Burgers, Roy Rogers's sandwich chain, and Kenny Rogers Roasters were born.

I'll never forget a speech I heard at a franchise forum in 1969 at Boston College. John Jay Hooker, Kentucky gubernatorial candidate and Minnie Pearl founder, had been regaling the audience with his love of franchising, recalling a conversation with his brother and business partner, Henry Hooker. "Henry," John Jay had said, "I just sold the state of Louisiana for $250,000, and it felt so good, I think I'm going to sell it all over again." It got a big laugh from the audience, but in my mind it was no laughing matter. I thought it was a scandal. Innocent people were losing their hard-earned savings buying into franchise systems that were not proven, that had not built a product or service with a competitive difference, and did not employ a distribution system or marketing strategy that would make for a flourishing business.

What many didn't understand was that it wasn't the name *McDonald's* that was responsible for such record-breaking success. Rather, it was a business system: their pioneering of a Henry Ford Model-T production line delivery system not only streamlined the process of creating delicious sandwiches inexpensively, but they had the ability to market them with the most sophisticated packaged goods methods known. This same ability to provide the consumer with better value and convenience was at the heart of the success of other franchise food chains like Kentucky Fried Chicken and Dunkin' Donuts.

The state and federal legislation that was being considered not only sought to end certain abuses but in some legislatures went so far as to discuss outlawing the system of franchising entirely. Both the automobile and petroleum dealers associations saw this as an opportunity to win long-sought-after legislation that would finally better their hand in dealing with their big corporate franchisors. Legislators were being urged to consider all offerings to be registered with the federal government, outlawing earnings claims, insuring required buybacks, and restricting new distribution in existing markets for fear it would impact existing franchises. They urged legislators to require automatic renewals of franchise agreements after the original term had expired.

So I found myself, as incoming chairman of the IFA, testifying and urging Congress—in countless hearings—to allow the association to put into effect its newly established code of conduct, in essence allowing us to police ourselves. Senator Philip Hart of Michigan was charged with fashioning national franchise legislation. It was he and his staff who ultimately decided to stay federal legislation in favor of the Federal Trade Commission setting national disclosure standards. The FTC established a universal registration statement that required of all franchisors a detailing of the offering, information about key executives and their backgrounds, earnings claims, and a ten-day cooling-off period between signing the contract and when it came in effect.

I also testified before the Small Business Administration. Their general counsel, Phil Zeidman, held hearings to restrict franchise systems from participating in government lending programs. Phil was a brilliant lawyer who would, in later days, after his tenure in government, become a close advisor, friend, and defender of our company. He, too, was convinced that the benefits of the franchising system outweighed the problems and, ultimately, stayed the hand of government from interfering.

CRISIS MANAGEMENT

Taking action wasn't my problem in those years. The fact is, I would have been far better off had I been more contemplative. My impetuousness and aspirations led me to spin my organization off in too many directions at once. Shades of my father.

In the midst of all the tumult, on the very night I assumed the chairmanship of the IFA, the part-time association managers in Chicago asked for an unsupportable increase in their retainer. I demurred; they resigned. Now I had to figure out how to position the association for the future. I decided to look at this as an opportunity to move from part-time association staffers in Chicago, who represented other associations in addition to ours, to our own full-time executive. And since most of the political action was in Washington, Phil Zeidman and I decided to move the offices of the IFA there from Chicago.

I hired Howard Rogerson, a former SBA executive in Washington, to be our first full-time executive director. I introduced Howard to our membership in meetings as we toured around the country. This was a major move for the IFA.

The following year, the IFA's executive committee raised the annual dues from $600 to $6,000 a year from each company, based on their revenue. We calculated that the association needed that kind of income if we were to afford the staff needed to do a proper job. Had we not received support from the membership, the association certainly could have folded at that time, but I'm happy to report that the organization thrives to this day.

I remember the first IFA meeting I attended in the summer of 1964. It was at O'Hare Airport, and the attendance was so small that we conducted the meeting around one round table. Today, the IFA's annual convention is attended by more than three thousand participants, and it is one of the nation's strongest trade associations.

In the sixty years since its founding, the Association has grown into a respected and effective force: in Washington, state capitals, and in selected international venues.

LESSON FOUR:
Suggestions for an Effective Planning Process

The Cheshire cat in Lewis Carroll's masterpiece, *Alice's Adventures in Wonderland,* uttered some of the wisest words I've ever heard. To paraphrase, the wise cat warned: *If you don't know where you are going, any road will take you there.*

To me, these words meant: whether it be a government, a family, a business, or an individual, if the entity does not have a clear plan as to what they want to be, what they want to have, and the four to six initiatives that will best take them there, the outcome is most likely to be very unsatisfactory.

Although the following lesson details a planning language and process in a business setting, the approach I propose can be applied, albeit less formally, in other settings with equally good results. For example, I propose as part of the planning process the involvement of a board of directors for review. The involvement of outsiders brings discipline and better effort to the process. But the review need not be as formal as what one might expect from a board of directors. A group of advisors who meet regularly could serve this purpose as well. In a family setting, a "kitchen cabinet" of a few trusted friends, whose opinion you value, could serve as a sounding board for your plans.

In the introduction to this book, I declared that one of the four major responsibilities of a leader is to steward strategy. The following are the language and steps I used to carry out this critical function.

There are numerous formulas and approaches to strategy creation. Many creative ideas are proposed by major strategy consulting firms like McKinsey or Boston Consulting Group. The approach I used and am suggesting here may not be the last word, but it has served me well over the years.

For me, it all begins with precise language and a clear and unchanging definition of terms.

•

For me, it all begins with precise language and a clear and unchanging definition of terms.

•

In my experience, terms like *vision, mission, objectives, goals, strategy,* and *tactics* can be misunderstood. I have seen these words not only employed differently from one executive to the next in the same company but used differently within a company from one planning cycle to the next. The upshot of this imprecise language most often leads to conflict, misery, misalignment, and failure. The solution is to have an agreed-upon definition of planning terms used consistently and understood throughout the enterprise.

1. Vision. *A vision is a statement about what the leadership agrees a company could reasonably stretch to be in a generation—a thirty-year aspiration.* If the statement doesn't contain the words *to be,* then it doesn't fulfill the requirement. For example, a thirty-year vision might be something like this: We wish to be the largest food service company in the United States as measured by sales within thirty years.

2. Mission Statement. *If a vision is what you want the business* to be *by the next generation, a* mission *is what you wish the company* to be *over the next three to five years.* This is the next step in strategy creation and, arguably, the most critical. It is here that leadership decides not only what they wish the enterprise *to be,* but just as importantly, what it will *not be.* This statement casts a spotlight over not only all the activities the company will and won't focus on but where resources will be allocated. So if the mission is to be *a diversified food service company,* the strategy of a portfolio of companies and the concept behind Universal Food Systems makes sense. But if the mission is to be *the dominant donut and coffee provider in each and every market in which you compete,* then an entirely different agenda is set for the organization. In my opinion if a mission is miscast, the best organization in the world can't save you.

Agreeing on a mission statement is hard work. It requires the CEO and his team to be absolutely realistic about its capabilities and about the competition it faces. Max Dupree, former CEO of the office equipment giant Herman Miller, wrote the 1987 book *Leadership Is an Art.* In it, he says the most important job of a CEO is to define reality. It is working through the mission statement where this notion of defining reality is most tested. The management needs to see the world and themselves as they really are, not as they wish to be.

They must know their customers and their competition cold. They must be able to see where they have or can build a sustainable competitive advantage. And no competitive advantage is sustainable indefinitely. Customers and competition are constantly changing, requiring management to revisit, on a regular basis, the subject of what you want to be.

3. Objectives. *If* Vision *and* Mission *are what you want* to be, *then objectives or goals (interchangeable terms in my lexicon) are what you want* to have. There are literally hundreds of activities one can measure in a business. Sales, costs, customer satisfaction measurements, return on investment, production utilization—the list is truly endless. At every level of the organization, there are a few goals that are most critical. These are the ones that most define success. I believe a group can keep their eye on no more than three to five objectives at a time. At the corporate level at Dunkin' Donuts, we selected three critical objectives we believed most defined success for our company.

Our objectives were:

- To have earnings per share grow at 15 to 20 percent per annum,
- To have shop-level economics achieve at least a 15 percent return on investment on average, and
- To have debt never amount to more than three times EBITDA (earnings before interest, taxes, depreciation, and amortization).

Other subentities in the company may select other measurements that best reflect achievement of their plans. For example, if one of the strategic initiatives of the overall company was to constantly improve customer satisfaction, the operation department's plan may call for one of its three to five objectives to be the improvement in customer satisfaction scores by 5 percent for the year.

4. Strategic Initiatives. *These are the four to six most important tasks an organization must execute in order to best bridge ever-scarce resources to achieve the stated objectives.* My belief is that every entity, even one as rich as the United States, has limited resources. Furthermore, it's my contention that no organization can effectively turn its attention to more than six major initiatives at a time. I have observed that if you ask an organization to pull more levers than that at any one time, none are executed well.

The responsibility for achieving each strategic initiative cascades down through the organization. For example, in our case, we decided the best way to achieve our 15 percent earnings per share goal—one of our six strategic initiatives—was to grow new distribution (new stores) by 3 percent per year. That translated to the real estate division having as one of their objectives the opening of one hundred new stores in the coming year. That department would then detail the four to six initiatives needed to accomplish this objective.

For example, they may decide their initiatives would be:

- Hire two additional real estate executives
- Open up three additional markets for development
- Upgrade their real estate brokerage network in four markets

5. Tactics. *The four to six action steps needed to support the achievement of each department's strategic initiative.* Tactics are a more granular look at the initiatives. As the objectives cascade down to the last level of the organization, tactics are what one must execute to ultimately get the job done. Again, using the real estate department as an example, the department might have an objective of opening a hundred stores in the coming year, but an individual real estate representative might be responsible for opening twenty of those shops in his geographic area. So a sample of his initiatives might look like this:

- Find a new broker to represent the brand on the north side of town.
- Work with three qualified franchise owners to expand in their areas.
- Arrange the purchase and remodel of two closed Kentucky Fried Chicken outlets to our brand.

THE CRUCIAL ROLE OF THE BOARD

I have found that an active and engaged board of directors, whether in a public or private company, dramatically raises the level of discipline and professionalism brought to the planning process. No question that management lifts their level of play when they know they will be presenting their plan to an outside board. Regarding the board's responsibilities, I believe strategic planning ranks second in importance only to their duty and authority either to retain or dismiss the CEO.

To help the board accomplish its core responsibilities, we established an annual agenda to address a rotating cycle of issues at each meeting throughout the year. Most boards meet four to six times a year and review a standard agenda of company concerns. Rather than just review the most recent financials and discuss issues as they occur, we decided that each of the four meetings should have its own focus.

In addition to the usual committee and financial reports, we decided that at our first meeting a full brand review should kick off our annual planning cycle. At this key meeting, the CEO or marketing chief would give an in-depth review of where we stood in comparison to our industry, including our competitors. It was a detailed assessment of our strengths, weaknesses, opportunities, and threats.[2] All the while, we used the lexicon *vision, mission, objectives,* and *strategic initiatives.* It was absolutely essential that everyone in the organization understood and was aligned with the plan going forward. This was particularly true of the board. These reviews were designed to raise essential strategic questions and give board members a chance to weigh in.

The second of our four meetings focused on a five-year plan. Within the context of a brand review, management put actual numbers to the plan. Again, this review gave all board members an opportunity to question the strategy.

The third meeting is designed to review the annual plan. It should dovetail to the five-year plan.

Finally, the fourth meeting of the year is dedicated to a review of the organization's "depth," defined as adequacy and promotability of key staff members. The CEO presents a review of each key executive's performance, ability, and time frame for promotion. It gives the board an opportunity to see how deep the management team is and forces a look at potential succession for every position, including the CEO.

Had that format focusing on strategy been in place, it is quite possible that the board might have caught me as I teetered on the slippery slope of mission creep. They might have pointed out the errors of my misguided change in mission and my devastatingly unsustainable objectives.

LESSON FIVE:
Importance of Striking the Right Balance between Exploitation and Experimentation

Michael Tushman, Harvard Business School organizational theorist and manuscript advisor, maintains that only a small fraction of businesses make it beyond forty years. To make it into that elite circle requires a certain amount of ambidexterity: the ability to simultaneously protect the core, yet experiment and adapt to an ever-changing marketplace. Too many or inappropriate changes or too few can spell the end of an enterprise. Achieving the right balance between exploration and exploitation is the art of leadership. I would contend that the creation of Universal Food Systems demonstrated that my dad and his team were ambidextrous. Unfortunately, I also believe they were seriously unbalanced. With eight separate businesses running the gamut from a small hamburger chain, to pancake houses and a delicatessen, they did a lot more exploration than their small and inexperienced management team could handle. By the same token, by not getting their arms around Dunkin' Donuts, the "diamond in the rough" in their midst—and getting it scalable—they were way too light on exploitation.

In this second era of my career, I, too, fell prey to miscalculating the balance between exploitation and experimentation. My impetuosity, arrogance, and lack of wisdom sent me spinning out new businesses under an expanded mission while simultaneously managing a trade association, expanding internationally to Japan, and engaging in the development of a novel donut-making machine. Not only were some of the activities misguided, but they were too numerous and far afield for my young and thinly manned organization to handle. It is little wonder the board was about to fire me. Fortunately, I saw the error of my ways in time. It is said one can learn a lot more from failure than success, if you can survive it. I know that's true in my case. This is a lesson I will never forget.

ERA 3: 1974–80

THE RESURRECTION

BACKGROUND

We return to the Dunkin' Donuts boardroom on that fateful April day in 1974. The board had been deliberating for about an hour before asking me to rejoin the meeting. They were deciding whether to fire me or give me another quarter to prove my claim that management had a handle on the problems and that it was only a matter of time before they were remedied.

That hour seemed like an eternity. I knew how disappointed the board members were and that a radical change might be coming at me fast. Just days before, my wife, Lorna, and I had been walking around our newly built home as we discussed conditions in the company and just what the future might hold for us. We loved our new house and had been there only a few years but were resigned—if things fell apart—to sell and begin anew.

I took a big breath and reentered the room. Bob Howard said the words I'd been hoping to hear: "Bob, we've discussed the matter and have decided to give you another quarter to see if you are, in fact, on the road to recovery."

•

"Bob, we've discussed the matter and have decided to give you another quarter to see if you are, in fact, on the road to recovery."

•

I let out a huge sigh of relief and told them they wouldn't regret their decision.

My confidence in the future was real. I believed we had realistically assessed the problems and that in fact most of the big issues had already been fixed. I was further—and probably most importantly—buoyed by my confidence in the team I'd gathered around me.

From the day he joined the company seven years earlier, Tom Schwarz had demonstrated his superior talent and capabilities. He quickly ramped up to administrative vice president, responsible for purchasing, design and construction, and human resources. A few years later, he moved up to executive vice president, responsible for all operations and administrative functions. I found myself increasingly turning to him for advice on all corporate matters.

My relationship with Tom was best summed up in a book by Michael Eisner, now retired CEO of Disney, titled *Working Together: Why Great Partnerships Succeed*. Ironically, Eisner suffered a reputation for having an ego bigger than all outdoors. His book tells a different tale, however. In it, he makes the point that behind most successful lives and companies you will not find just one driving force but most often two. He details how colleagues who like, respect, and complement each other's talents not only bring out the best in each other but the best for the company. Eisner posits that "partnerships built on friendship, devoid of envy, jealousy, and rivalry, are the best pathway to success."[1]

Eisner tells the story of how Stanley Gold, Roy Disney's representative, made it a condition of Eisner assuming the CEO role at Disney that he would co-CEO with a relative stranger, Frank Wells. Frank was a lawyer and former head of Warner Brothers. When Eisner balked at the notion of co-CEOs, Frank graciously agreed to be chief operating officer. That began a friendship and symbiotic relationship that would last ten years until Frank's untimely death in a helicopter crash in April 1994. Eisner details what it was like to work with someone who not only protected the organization but him as well, someone who advised him and supported him and did it all selflessly. That ten-year partnership will be remembered as the halcyon days of Disney's miraculous turnaround. Problems sprung up at Disney right after Frank's death. First, Jeffrey Katzenberg, the very talented head of animation, left followed by the incredibly costly and public failure associated with the hiring and firing of Michael Ovitz, the short-lived chief operating officer.

Eisner goes on to tell of ten other notable partnerships and their successes: well-known alliances such as Warren Buffett and Charlie Munger, Bill and Melinda Gates, and in baseball, Joe Torre and Don Zimmer. He recounts the stories of pairs who are similar, tales of duos who differ radically in manner and temperament, partners of similar age and those born decades apart, loud and colorful characters aligned with modest and withdrawn figures. For all the contrasts, there is one common thread: these are people who love what they do and have found that true partnerships create happiness.

I felt I had that same winning relationship with Tom. In the book *The Winning Performance: How America's High-Growth Midsize Companies Succeed*, the authors state: "At Dunkin' Donuts, the marketing and strategic skills of Bob Rosenberg go together with the finance and administrative wizardry of Tom Schwarz like . . . coffee and doughnuts."[2] In reality, the lines were a little fuzzier, since we both possessed those skills, but the fact remains that we were partners in all matters. I cannot think of a major decision made where we didn't agree. Good times and bad, successes or failures, we shared laughter and tears—never recriminations or finger pointing.

That feeling of comradeship and trust extended to the next nine in command.[3] I never felt diminished or threatened by my teammates' skills or ideas—just the opposite. In fact, I was comforted to be surrounded by such incredible talent. My confidence stemmed from my belief that there was no problem or issue so great that we couldn't solve or get through it together.

STRATEGY

After realizing the error of our ways, we closed the three fish and chip shops and ceased looking for other concepts to franchise. We also abandoned and wrote off our forays into both the automated donut equipment and frozen pies project. We closed nearly a hundred of the worst-performing shops and wrote off the prospective real estate costs attendant to those closings.

In 1974, we launched our first new product since Jumbo Java: the now world-famous donut hole treats called Munchkins®. Like so many good ideas that improved our business, this one came from a franchise owner.

For years at Halloween we'd collect the donut holes produced from our first-cut cake donuts, put them in cellophane bags—very much like potato chip bags—and showcase them on the counter in clip-on displays. We'd leave them plain or roll them in powdered or cinnamon sugar. We thought they made a good trick-or-treat item. These donut holes sold quite well the week or two before the holiday.

In the spring of '73, I got a call from one of our most successful franchise owners, Bob Demery. He said, "You have to come down and see what Edna has done!" Bob and his wife, Edna, owned two stores in Hartford, Connecticut. Rather than collect donut holes left over from the cutting, Edna had made a new cutter that yielded a larger product, each one-fifth of a regular donut size. She made both yeast and cake and finished them like regular donuts; some had fruit fillings and others she honey-dipped. She devoted the entire front showcase to these new kind of donut holes, piled high. His voice full of excitement, Bob added, "They're selling like crazy. Our business is up 20 percent!"

It wasn't more than a day or two later when Tom and I, with our marketing head in tow, paid Hartford a visit. Sure enough, it was exactly as Demery had said. We knew then and there we had the making of a big winner.

We viewed this as a special project and retained Hill Holiday and Cosmopolis, at the time a small advertising agency. They had done a very good job a number of years earlier with our aborted hamburger chain, Howdy Beef n' Burger. We liked them and believed Steve Cosmopolis, the creative partner, was very talented. Cosmopolis's first suggestion was to call these new treats "Penny Poppers." We were intrigued and sat with the idea for a while but eventually believed inflation was at hand and we'd never be able to hold the line on a penny per donut hole.

In those years, CBS would play the 1939 classic *The Wizard of Oz* annually, which of course featured the Munchkins, the little people who inhabited the land of Oz. Hill Holiday and Cosmopolis thought the name was a natural and pushed to see who owned the rights. They discovered that Jack's Cookie Company in Louisiana had trademarked the name. Archie Southgate, an attorney and board member, was recruited to reach out to Jack's and see what could be done to use the name for our donut holes. As it turned out, Jack's had yet to find a use for Munchkins® and Archie leased the name for a dollar a year.

The agency created Maxfield Parrish–like characters to adorn our boxes—little people shown making and finishing the donuts a la the Lilliputians from *Gulliver's Travels*. We had package sizes of ten and twenty, and buckets of thirty. And, of course, a customer could buy any number if they chose.

We launched our ad campaign, as luck would have it, during the great oil embargo of 1974. Despite the long lines waiting for gas on odd- and even-numbered days and the frayed tempers that went along with it, our introduction of Munchkins® was a smashing success. Our same-store sales skyrocketed by more than 12 percent. Not since the introduction of Jumbo Java had we seen such industry-topping sales performance.

But undoubtedly, the biggest sea change in the company came about as a result of answering a question posed by one of our board members, Archie Southgate: "What would the world look like if you really slowed down new-store openings? What if you focused your time, money, and attention on strengthening the existing shops?" In all honesty, my first reaction was that such a change in strategy would throw an unacceptable crimp in our earnings growth.

But I liked and respected Archie, and his question kept cropping up in my thoughts, so much so that I soon felt compelled to provide him with a decent answer.

Years before, while in graduate school, I had become familiar with Jay Forrester's work at MIT on simulation, a new technology that allowed one to model a company's performance under a wide array of assumptions. Our head of computer operations was Tom Johnson, who, as luck would have it, was an MIT grad. I approached Tom about whether he could build such a model. Before I knew it,

I had a tool by which our team could make strategic assumptions about our growth in same-store sales, general and administrative expenses, new-store growth, and profit margins of company-owned shops. This indispensable tool could model our earnings growth with tremendous accuracy and would become part of our semiannual strategy reviews for decades to come.

And, lo and behold, I could now answer Archie's question with a great degree of certitude. The model demonstrated that, in fact, we could reduce growth from 140 new stores a year to just 40 [to pair with the 140 . . .]. With some reallocation and reduction in overhead coupled with modest assumptions about same-store sales growth, we could grow earnings per share for many years at a 15 to 20 percent clip. The result? We refocused our *mission* and reduced our *objective* to a much safer and much more achievable rate.

ORGANIZATION

With a slower growth strategy, we decided to drop our decentralized form of organization. We would keep our regional presence, using smaller offices to service our operational supervisors in the field, but bring back to headquarters our best executives to head up a now-functional organization. Ralph Gabellieri, who had moved his family from Rhode Island to Texas at great personal sacrifice to solve our problems there, returned to headquarters to helm franchise operations. And just as he had done in Rhode Island a decade previous, Ralph fixed the problems: he closed some low-performing stores, moved other poor performers into stronger franchise hands, and uplifted the region through better operations.

We strengthened our team with some new hires as well. When Tom Schwarz was promoted from his position as head of human resources, he recruited Rick Power as his replacement. Rick was a talented executive and an excellent athlete who played baseball on the Williams College team and was, for a time, a pro prospect. Tom recruited Rick from General Electric, where he worked in the human resources department.

Tom also hired Sid Feltenstein as regional VP in the Mid-Atlantic zone. When we reorganized, Sid assumed responsibility for company-owned store operations. After graduation from Boston University, Sid had gone to work for Procter and Gamble as a management trainee, then to the Speidel Watch Company, finally helping to create the Candy Corporation of America. Sid would prove to be a transformational player in our company's fortunes.

The most unusual, and I'd say extraordinary, of these hires, was that of Larry Hantman as vice president and general counsel. After Jack Alpert's sudden and untimely death, I had decided to bring our legal function in house. I had been sitting in my office worrying about the growing list of litigation in which we were embroiled, mentally paging through all the lawyers I knew who might be able to bail us out of our legal nightmare. I lit upon Larry Hantman, one of my old fraternity brothers at Cornell. Although we lived in different off-campus housing, we ate lunch and dinner together every day. I remembered Larry's wry sense of humor and keen intellect. "Larry would be perfect," I thought. "I wonder where he is now and whether he'd have any interest. . . ."

Within an hour, Rick Power, our human resources chief, stopped by my office to tell me he'd just gotten off the phone with a local headhunter who'd spoken with an old friend of mine. "He spoke to a Larry Hantman," Rick said. "Larry is at Tyco, and although he doesn't want to put any pressure on an old friend, he asked if he could speak with you." I was dumbfounded. I don't believe in divine intervention, but nothing like this has happened to me before or since.

We lost no time arranging a lunch meeting, and I offered Larry the job on the spot. He left Tyco and became one of my most trusted advisors and closest friends. I have always considered this turn of events a godsend. The company never had another significant legal controversy from the day he joined to the day I retired.

After enduring 1969 to 1973, a brutal five-year stretch, I was convinced that we had finally put together a superb organization. We had amassed a complementary group of individuals who liked and respected one another and an appropriate strategy and set of sound objectives that would serve our company for years to come. These strong elements gave me confidence in my promise to the board that the worst was behind us and that they would have no reason to regret their decision to keep me on board.

COMMUNICATION

During those trying years, other activities had gotten in the way of implementing a communications program for both our own executive team and our franchise owners. In the end, there was a fearful price to pay for that omission.

We were embroiled in a class action suit brought by nine franchise owners that had the potential to destroy the company. In addition, a few franchisees had instigated a movement to form their own union.

My first reaction was anger. In my eyes, many of these franchise owners were ingrates and were acting out of line. After all, they were among the most successful in our system and were on their way to riches they might have never achieved had it not been for the Dunkin' Donuts system.

But that view changed drastically one night as I sat ensconced in my favorite chair in my living room reading a book just penned by David Halberstam titled *The Best and The Brightest*. Halberstam told the story of the failures of the Kennedy and Johnson administrations in their management of the Vietnam War. As he saw it, the war was being waged on our part by smart Harvard- and Yale-educated managers like Robert McNamara and McGeorge Bundy. Those leaders were "the best and the brightest" our country had to offer, but they suffered from what Halberstam called "hubris," a Greek word for arrogance. They relied on statistics and information supplied from the field and their own insights. Regrettably, they never traveled to the towns and hamlets in Vietnam. They never talked to the community leaders on the front lines in an attempt to understand the facts and the real issues. As a result, the United States was losing the hearts and minds of the South Vietnamese citizens, and losing the war.

That's when lightning struck. *Oh my God, Halberstam could be just as well be talking about us.* The very next day, I shared my insights with Tom and the team, and we began to fashion a remedy.

First and foremost, we decided that when problems occur, we would never blame the followership but rather assume that the fault lay with the leadership. We would take on 100 percent of the responsibility.

Next, we agreed that we would institute a store-visitation program in which each of our ten senior managers, including myself, would travel to at least one hundred stores per year. We would visit with district managers and get to know them and their issues. That first year I visited 113 stores seeking coffee, donuts, and ideas. These meetings gave us the chance to talk individually with each store owner in his or her own shop. Finally, we resolved to devote one of our monthly senior leadership (operating committee) meetings each quarter to sharing our findings.

This program yielded countless wonderful benefits. For one, it provided priceless insights into how to improve our system. For another, it gave us an opportunity to demonstrate our respect and recognition of the importance of skilled, knowledgeable district managers and store owners. Time is the most precious asset; it took us a while as a company to realize that spending it with our franchisees was not time lost.

In my travels, I would habitually ask the district manager about his objectives and strategies for his district. This gave me a direct window into whether our management-by-objectives language was making its way through every layer of the business. My two favorite questions for the franchise owners were: "If you had the opportunity to invest in this Dunkin' Donuts franchise today, would you do it all over again?" and "If you were CEO of this company, what would you do differently?"

We always would announce our visits in advance, since the purpose wasn't to surprise and spot check for service, cleanliness, and quality but to communicate. We already had an inspection system in place that would measure those aspects of our business. And to our trained eye, even if the appointment was announced, we could reasonably assess how closely our operating standards were being met.

Another outgrowth of my aha! moment was our newfound commitment to breathe life into our moribund advisory council system. Years earlier, in an attempt to improve communication between franchise owners and company management, we had established an advisory council of franchisee leaders as identified and appointed by the company. They were to regularly meet with senior company leadership, or that was the intention; in reality it was administered in a haphazard way and didn't serve a useful purpose.

We concluded that the need for people of similar interests to meet and have input was a very normal human need. We had to look no further than the Rotary, Lions, or chambers of commerce in every community to see evidence of our conclusion. Ultimately, we realized that if we didn't fashion this organized system to air grievances and share collective wisdom, the franchise owners would create it themselves.

The system we created gave each store one vote to elect a district representative. Along with the district manager, each district representative would chair the regular district meetings. Each district manager supervised twenty to thirty stores. The district chair and cochair would attend quarterly advisory meetings in each of our five geographic regions: New England, Mid-Atlantic, Southeast, Midwest, and West. These meetings would be held with the regional vice president. Each quarter, the chair and cochair of each of the five regions would meet with senior management at the home office.

To ensure that the meetings at district, regional, and national levels didn't devolve into impromptu complaint sessions, we worked with franchise leadership to agree on a per-store annual earnings improvement objective as a focus for the meetings. The agendas were designed to look at strategic initiatives at each level, all with the goal of meeting the earnings improvement objectives. That is not to say we would not discuss contract modifications, but we would only do so in the context of how they might affect overall store profitability. This proved to be a powerful way to make contract modifications that improved the system dramatically. We also used the input from national and regional representatives on task forces to help us design needed improvements in the system. These owners provided invaluable input on future store designs, additional advertising, new products, and improved distribution systems.

Though we attempted to train both our district managers and franchise leadership on how to conduct meetings, we weren't as successful there as we had hoped. We realized that when it came to group dynamics, the appointed leader might not be the person the group turned to for guidance. In some cases, the district manager was simply not as competent as the franchisee the district elected as its leader. Therefore, we set about to identify and train both.

Part of that training was to sensitize everyone to the importance of setting an intention for the type of conversations that were to be held in a meeting. For example, certain meetings can be characterized as information only: designed just to brief the group, say, on average profit and loss data for the district. Other dialogues might focus on brainstorming: a free-form exchange of ideas, with no decisions expected, discussing, for example, new product ideas. Then there are the powwows created expressly for decision-making, such as nailing down just what advertising promotion will be selected for the next quarter. We also trained all participants to use our strategy-planning language and format to keep the group on track.

CRISIS MANAGEMENT

Clearly the greatest threat to the enterprise in this era was the class action suit brought against the company. Class action suits were very much in vogue in the 1970s. These suits enabled one or a few plaintiffs to make a claim on behalf of a whole class of potential litigants. A judge's determination of a class was predicated on whether common issues predominate in the case or, conversely, whether potential claimants had a different and individual basis for their claim.

A battery of "strike lawyers" emerged who would take these cases "on a contingency"—a slice of the damages. It was an enticing incentive. If a class was determined, the leverage—based on potential damages—was so great most defendants would settle, often for huge sums. The plaintiffs' lawyers were, for the most part, entitled to one-third of the judgment or settlement.

In 1972, nine past and present franchise owners filed a treble damage suit alleging violations of the Sherman Antitrust Act. They sought damages of $80 million and injunctive relief. At the time, the company stock was at an all-time low, the total market capitalization sitting at no more than $40 million. The plaintiffs asked Judge Edward Becker, a federal judge in the Third Circuit's District Court for the Eastern District of Pennsylvania, to find whether a class existed. They claimed the company engaged in a tie, compelling franchisees to buy equipment and lease real estate from the company in order to acquire the franchise. If true, this would have constituted a per se violation of the antitrust laws and entitle the aggrieved party treble damages.

The Third Circuit was known as a very friendly plaintiffs' jurisdiction. A short while before, General Electric and a few of their competitors had lost a major price-fixing case in that federal district, resulting in heavy prison sentences and huge damage payments. The plaintiffs in the Dunkin' Donuts case had selected the Berger Law firm in Philadelphia, a well-known strike firm and one of the winning firms in the GE suit.

Many of the plaintiffs were well known to me. Some of the nine were among our most successful franchise owners in the Mid-Atlantic region. I never spoke to them about their motivations in launching the suit. But I long suspected they saw the company in a weakened state and saw their actions as a way to take ownership of the system. Some of the leaders of the suit owned large stock positions in the company.

In any event, we were sure of our innocence. Several years previous, we had separated our $15,000 initial franchise fee from the $35,000 equipment package. As a result, as long as the equipment met our standards, we were totally indifferent as to where the prospective franchisee purchased it. In addition, we had only engaged in leasing and subleasing real estate to franchisees because, for the most part, they could not get financing for the real estate on their own. We had long before concluded that real estate provided a far poorer return than issuing a franchise, which had an almost infinite rate of return. If a franchise owner could finance his real estate without our credit, we would have been thrilled. In those early years, the '50s and '60s, we were in the real estate business as a means to prime the pump, to build the brand for the day when franchisees could finance growth on their own.

So, regarding these suits, we felt confident that the truth would come out. We believed we'd easily be exonerated based on our contracts and practices. The well-regarded law firm of Pepper, Hamilton, and Sheetz in Philadelphia represented us, while our attorney on the case was their antitrust expert, Alfred "Chub" Wilcox.

Larry Hantman was charged with the job of overseeing our defense. He had already demonstrated his skill and value at settling a stockholder suit in New York and other litigation he had inherited. He reviewed all of Wilcox's briefs and did a good amount of his own writing in our defense as well. Despite our innocence and Wilcox's assurance that there was no basis at all for a class finding, the potential outcome was so potentially cataclysmic that I found myself overseeing each step in the process.

Plaintiff's counsel was quite shrewd. In the hearing before Judge Becker, the Berger firm paraded a group of franchisees, all of whom aired their complaints. I was becoming concerned about the tone that the hearings were taking. I couldn't help thinking, "A judge is human, too, and quite possibly he may be swayed by some of the hard-luck stories he's heard." But Wilcox was reassuring. "He's too smart for that," he'd said. "We don't need any testimony to refute; we can rely on our contracts and the law."

Most of us can remember where we were and what we were doing when life-altering events like JFK's death or the 9/11 attacks occurred. Along with those dates, March 12, 1975, is one I will never forget. That is the day that Judge Becker issued his ruling; it was also the day I had invited Ron Joyce, owner of the Tim Hortons donut chain, to our offices to discuss the possibility of buying his chain.

It was a rainy afternoon—a bad omen already. I met Ron in my office. As we were exchanging pleasantries, Lee Shultz, my administrative assistant, interrupted to let us know that Chub Wilcox was on the phone and needed to speak to me right away. I had a sinking feeling. Wilcox told me Judge Becker had declared a class and that all current franchise owners were included. To not be included, a franchisee would have to petition the court (opt out). The judge actually wrote in his decision, "Where there is smoke there is fire." Though he acknowledged that exceptions in dealings with each of the plaintiffs existed, this made no difference. I felt like someone had hit me over the head with a sledgehammer.

I told Ron Joyce what had just happened and excused myself. He said he understood. It was like I was walking in a dream. My stomach was churning. I got in my car and drove the half hour to my home, went upstairs to my bathroom, and vomited.

It was the worst possible outcome. An $80 million threat hung over the head of the company. Until adjudicated, which could take years, the decision would, I believed, dramatically affect our stockholders and our relationship with our franchise owners. It seemed clear to me—just as I had feared—that Judge Becker had reached his decision based on emotions rather than our practices and the facts.

The following morning, I called a meeting to discuss next steps. My dad, Archie Southgate, Tom Schwarz, and Larry Hantman were all in attendance. The first decision was to remove Chub Wilcox as lead attorney and replace him with Phil Zeidman.

I had first met Phil when he was general counsel of the Small Business Administration. Phil grew up in Birmingham, Alabama, graduated Yale as a scholar of the first rank, attended Harvard Business School, and finally graduated from Harvard Law School. After becoming special assistant to Hubert Humphrey, this country's thirty-eighth vice president, Phil went into private practice in Washington, DC, swiftly becoming known as the best franchise lawyer in the world.

My friendship with Phil began when I testified before the SBA in the 1960s, and we grew even closer during my chairmanship of the IFA, when we moved the association headquarters from Chicago to Washington. Dunkin' Donuts had Phil and his firm on retainer at the time. He was one of the smartest people I had ever known, and I had turned to him for counsel on a wide variety of matters before this litigation.

I called Phil that fateful March afternoon, explained what had happened, and asked him if he wouldn't take the case as we sought to overturn the decision in the Third Circuit Court of Appeals. To my great relief, he agreed; and Larry, Phil, and I began work on our appeal.

A short time after Judge Becker's decision, George Mandell, my brother-in-law and a very successful Dunkin' Donuts franchise owner, began an effort to convince other franchisees to opt out of the class. George had originally trained as a pharmacist, but soon after I became CEO of Universal Food Systems in 1963, George—with a small loan from me and my father-in-law—left his pharmacy job and bought his first Dunkin' Donuts store in Dorchester, Massachusetts. The man was a natural. He went on to build or buy five more locations over the next seven years.

George was not only my brother-in-law but also one of my dearest friends and yet another trusted advisor. Counting all the grandparents, parents, and children, our family unit now numbered twelve, so between birthdays and anniversaries we'd enjoy a family party just about every other week. These were not only occasions to celebrate but also opportunities for George to brief me on what was happening on the front lines and share franchise-owner reaction to our policies. His judgment was superb and his input invaluable.

I was barred by a gag order from discussing the litigation with our franchisees. George was aware of my limitations but took it upon himself to reach out to other franchise leaders in an effort to save the company. The goal was to convince franchise owners to opt out of the class. At their own expense, George and the franchise leaders set up phone banks, reaching out to franchise owners all over the country, explaining how it was in the franchisees' best interest to defeat the class. Without a strong parent company, they argued, their operations would suffer and the value of their franchises would diminish.

Larry, Tom, and I traveled to Philadelphia to attend Phil's argument before the three-judge panel in the Court of Appeals. Phil was absolutely brilliant that day, and we left court and flew back to Boston glowing with confidence that the judges had been moved by Phil's arguments and the briefs he, Larry, and Arthur Cantor, another lawyer in Phil's office, had composed. But it's never over until it's over; I knew that.

March 4, 1976.

Another day I will never forget, and not because it was my thirty-eighth birthday. I was skiing at Loon Mountain in New Hampshire when I got the call from Larry. The Court of Appeals had just handed down their decision. They had overturned Judge Becker's decision three to zip and wrote an opinion that fully vindicated us, laying bare the errors in Judge Becker's earlier ruling. I was deliriously happy. It was as if a thousand-pound weight had been lifted off of my shoulders. Best birthday of my life.

It wasn't just that the financial threat had been lifted. Of course that was huge, but I was also overjoyed that our franchisees had been able to convince other owners to opt out, that they had been able to convey the wrongheadedness of this suit, and had demonstrated that we were not the evil franchisors we had been painted to be. When the final results of the class were tallied, fully 60 percent of our franchise owners had petitioned the court to opt out. Though I don't follow these matters closely, I would guess that is a record, and by a very wide margin.

When I reflect on this trying time and our victory, the only sad memory is the premature passing of my brother-in-law, George. He was taken by cancer at a young age. In his honor, the Dunkin' Donuts franchisees, the company, and suppliers established a yearly "George Mandell Annual Golf Tournament" for the Dana Farber Cancer Institute. Over the years, they have raised tens of millions of dollars in George's name: a fitting tribute to one of the great heroes in the Dunkin' Donuts story.

LESSON SIX:
My Take on the Tasks and Character of an Effective CEO

As I worked at my job, I thought a good deal about what tasks and qualities were important to be a good leader or CEO. The following are my conclusions:

1. Strategy: The CEO is the steward of the strategic direction of the enterprise. This critical function is to ensure that senior management defines not only the existing competitive advantage the company enjoys but where and how further sustainable competitive advantage can be discovered and built. The CEO, in concert with his or her senior management, decides what the company should be and—just as importantly—*what it will not be.* Easily said, but this deceptively simple process requires realistic assessments as well as vigorous and continuous monitoring and adjustment, since both the competition and the consumer are constantly changing. This kind of continual monitoring requires the CEO to know on an intimate level the strengths and weaknesses of his or her company as well as its competitors. A comprehensive knowledge of the industry in which the company competes is crucial to success. My store visits combined with my leadership roles in trade associations like the International Franchise Association and the National Restaurant Association were helpful to me in this regard.

2. Organization: The CEO bears the responsibility of recruiting and retaining talent with the requisite skills and abilities to execute the company strategy. As my guide to assessing and manning the organization, I relied heavily on the teachings of Peter Drucker, famed demographer, business writer, and teacher. In filling a job, Drucker would stress, it's best first to define the assignment in detail, then recruit and evaluate against the requirements of that assignment. But it is important to be limber as well. As the business changes, so do the assignments and, quite possibly, so does the search for the proper person to fill the job.

Another principal that guided me in manning the organization I learned from the Gallup Research Company and their work in organizational development. At its core, Gallup contends that everyone has strengths and weaknesses. They further believe it is very difficult, if not impossible, to remediate someone's weaknesses. They argue that the more effective way to build a high-functioning organization is to build on an individual's strengths, compensating weaknesses with other teammates who possess complementary strengths.

Key to this concept is that each teammate accepts that there is no shame in not being the best at everything. The team understands and celebrates the complementarity of their skills and aptitudes. Our team was composed of people with varying backgrounds and educational levels, but we shared a respect and trust in each other.

Selecting, coaching, and balancing the team takes a lot of time, but in my experience, recruiting and retaining the right organization ranks right up there with strategy as the most important and controlling factor in the success of an enterprise.

3. Communication: As CEO, you are the Communicator in Chief. The responsibility for aligning all the various constituencies in the organization behind company strategy falls primarily to the CEO, but it doesn't stop there. Just when you think you have communicated clearly to all parties, go back over your message again and again. You cannot make your point too clearly or check back enough times to make sure that everyone in your organization has not only understood your message but *buys into it as well*. The company mission bears repeating, sometimes ad nauseum. Most constituents are busy—sometimes overwhelmed—with their own responsibilities, and the message often doesn't sink in until you have reviewed and repeated it countless times.

4. Crisis Management: The last task on my CEO list. The world is stochastic. Unexpected events—often large and impactful—occur in business as in life. This can affect an enterprise in meaningful ways, requiring the CEO's concerted, and at times, immediate attention and management. First, I would direct my attention to matters that I thought affected the survivability of the business, a condition that , in my opinion, is the foremost responsibility of management. The tests I would use to determine where and when to intervene were:

- Materiality: When the dollar amount of the decision under consideration is large enough to impact the earnings of the company in a quarter by 10 percent.
- Scope: When the decision in question affects many people or multiple departments within the organization.

- Futurity: When the decision creates changes that are of significant size and commit the company many years into the future.

I often joked that being a CEO was like being a sailboat captain. At the helm at sea you experience many moments of calm, but they are punctuated by moments of sheer terror when you have to tack. And tacking is what a CEO is often called upon to do in certain critical moments.

QUALITIES

I have found that being a successful CEO not only depends on what you do but, just as importantly, who you are: what you value and how you behave. First, I believe he or she has to possess a real passion for the business and for their role in it. Second, it is essential that a leader be trusted. Trust is at the heart of all lasting and successful relationships and a subject I will deal with more thoroughly in the next lesson. Integrity, humility, and empathy are also key characteristics a leader must possess in order to be successful over the long term. *The US Army Leadership Field Manual* lists many of these very same qualities as well.

In addition, good and lasting leaders are driven by a goal greater than just making money. In my experience, the most enduring enterprises are driven by a vision and belief that the business brings real and important benefits to the world.

STYLE

In the business press, you often hear about two distinct styles, often diametrically opposed, as models for leadership success. The first is the autocratic leader, a person who rules supreme over all others in the organization. As leader, he or she makes most of the decisions and only relies on staff to implement them. We have all seen such leaders in history, in business, and in public life. I guess an argument can be made that there may be times in a company's life, or in certain circumstances, where the decisive and quick action of an autocrat is required. But I believe that sort of leadership can only be successful, if at all, for a very brief period.

I believe a model known as "servant leadership" is the more effective and lasting one. Here, a leader works to serve his or her people. The leader works to create a culture in which power is shared and the needs of the staff, not the leader, are put first. It is an environment where people are encouraged to create and lead as well as implement. Under this leadership style, the ingenuity and energy of the entire organization are more fully unlocked, resulting in higher performance. It is also a culture in which the leader takes the pain when things go badly (doesn't blame others) and shares the credit when things go well.

LESSON SEVEN:
The Importance of Trust and Mood in Coordinating Action

Over the years, I was fortunate to have many "teachers." These include actual teachers, as well as authors and colleagues who provided insights and lessons just when I and the company needed them most.

Fernando Flores, the minister of finance in the Allende regime in Chile, was one such teacher. He had been imprisoned for several years when General Pinochet came to power. Following his release, championed by Amnesty International, he came to the United States and completed his PhD at Berkeley. It was then that Flores started a company called Business Design Associates, or BDA, in order to teach the connection between language and actions. I was introduced to Flores and his teachings by my brother, Donald, and his wife at the time, Terry, who urged me to attend Flores's seminars. She had worked for Flores and BDA for five years as a coach and consultant. It was by attending these seminars that I began to more fully understand how powerful semantics can be in coordinating action between people. Among the many concepts Flores posits is that we, as humans, create ourselves in language. And that most of us are not very rigorous about the language we use, suffering enormously as a result.

Flores contends that trust is key in all relationships. It exists in all successful relationships and is absent in all failed or faltering ones. He provides four measurable standards to determine if trust exists. He argues that if trust is given too soon, one is naïve, but withheld too long, one runs the risk of becoming a cynic. Trust should be given or withheld based upon one's observations of the following four standards.

1. The first is *sincerity*. According to Flores, sincerity exists when: "private and public conversations are the same." In other words, one does not say one thing to people's faces while telling a different story behind their backs. In the case of our franchise owners, there was only one story. We wanted and needed them to be successful and to earn a fair return for the risk and hard work they put in. I believe they came to understand we were sincere in this regard.

2. The second standard is *competence*. Competence is not the same as never making a mistake; rather it is the notion that one performs up to the standards for the job in question. So if one is a commercial pilot, the standard is being able to get your passengers to their destination safe and sound, even if you have to make midcourse corrections. If you are a CEO, some mistakes are tolerable, but you are expected to consistently achieve the objectives to which you are committed. If not, you will be considered not up to the task or incompetent to do the job. I believe our franchise owners voted our management not perfect, but competent to do the job.

3. The third standard of trust is *reliability*. Reliability occurs when one competently manages one's promises, completing them on time and satisfactorily. If the person is unable to deliver as promised, due to extenuating circumstances, counteroffers are made, which may be either accepted or declined.

4. The fourth standard of trust is *care.* Care is evidenced when someone is committed to another's well-being over time, to his or her identity and future. People are seen and treated not as agents in a transactional sense, as someone who will serve our interests, but with a commitment to mutual satisfaction. This quality of *care* engenders partnership and intimacy, people working together creating a future. Even when circumstances require that someone be let go, it is done with respect and with an appreciation for the value of the relationship.

In retrospect, I see all four of these standards at play in the franchise owners' unprecedented decision to opt out of the class action law suit.

We promised our franchise owners a business system that, if followed faithfully, would be capable of delivering a fair return. When we became too preoccupied with opening new stores and not tending the system properly, we apologized, took full responsibility, and built an advisory system. We invited the franchisees in to help us fix it. In the process, I believe we demonstrated that we cared. Their vote in the class action lawsuit demonstrated their belief that we did as well.

Flores also sensitized me to the importance mood plays in people's attitudes and consequently their actions.

He said that moods are transitory; that they come and go, that *they are only an interpretation of the future.* If that is true, then one can design a mood by virtue of how one defines the future.

If you are anxious, afraid, hopeless, or resentful, your mood will reflect those attitudes. By the same reasoning, if your interpretation of the future is hopeful and optimistic, your mood will mirror those sunny thoughts. A lot has to do with the language you use as you think about the future.

Leaders have an immense impact on the mood of their company and their followership. As a leader, you are being observed, often in minute detail, by everyone in your organization. Your words, even your body language, are clues and are all interpreted—particularly in tough times. If you cannot see your way to extricating your organization out of a morass, if you have no confidence in your plan or your people, then it is time to leave. Your spoken word and body language will soon reflect this truth. Your optimism and confidence in the future must be realistic to be believed. If your plans and interpretation of the future are not grounded or realistic, that, too, will soon be discovered.

Authenticity is the coin of the realm and everyone involved will be looking for it and measuring you for it.

•

Authenticity is the coin of the realm and everyone involved will be looking for it and measuring you for it.

•

And, of course, people are astoundingly perceptive. In my own case, my promise to the board about our future was truly grounded, and I believed in it to my very core. I think that is the reason I was able to convince them to stick with me just a little bit longer.

ERA 4: 1980–83

HAPPY DAYS ARE HERE AGAIN

BACKGROUND

One would think with the class action lawsuit won, an effective strategy and organizational format, more than nine hundred profitable stores, and four years of rebounding earnings at more than 30 percent compounded, we would be free from worry.

But you'd be wrong.

I think worry was part of our DNA. Perhaps a part of every company's DNA? Perhaps it is even a survival mechanism in itself. Competitive and committed to winning, we were constantly looking ahead, scanning the competition, and taking the temperature of an ever-changing consumer.

In 1978, Mister Donut—now under International Multifoods— had more than six hundred shops, two hundred of which were in Japan. After a few years of false starts, this once fierce competitor hired a new CEO named Dick Niglio to head up their brand.

Niglio was smart and aggressive. An All-East fullback at Yale, Dick had been a CEO of a franchise company before taking the Mister Donut assignment. Since Mister Donut headquarters was still in the Boston area, Niglio moved there and became a neighbor and friend. We'd play tennis, socialize, and travel with our wives to trade association meetings. The competition on the tennis court, though friendly, was just as fierce as it was professionally. In the trade press, Niglio proclaimed, "Our objective is to be the largest donut operation in the world, and we hope to accomplish this in the next five years."[1]

These were fighting words!

●

These were fighting words!

●

But in truth, competition was everywhere.

Winchell's was a regional donut shop franchisor established in the West, now expanding as far eastward as Chicago. By 1978, Winchell's had 850 shops in sixteen states.

The founder, Verne Winchell, had sold his company to Denny's and soon became CEO of the holding company responsible for both brands. Winchell boasted in the trade press: "Winchell's was first in profitability of any donut shop chain in the world, and planned to rapidly expand their chain eastward."[2]

In Canada, Ron Joyce (Tim Hortons) was becoming a formidable competitor as well. But his growth was not limited to Canada: he began to expand over the border into Buffalo and Rochester, even into southern Florida.

Despite our inauspicious first meeting on the day of our class action verdict, Ron and I developed an ongoing friendship. From time to time, he would have me up to his home in Hamilton, Ontario, it seemed with the sole intention of teasing me with the prospect of selling us his business.

In 1976, McDonald's introduced the Egg McMuffin and was emerging as a powerful competitor for the morning fast-food consumer. Previously, all McDonald's stores opened for business at 11:00 a.m. With the addition of breakfast, they were now opening at 6:00 or 7:00 a.m. and, with all their advertising dollars, threatened to change the competitive landscape. It is important to note here that the average Dunkin' Donuts shop racked up 50 percent of its sales by 11:00 a.m.

As we were facing this barrage of expanding retail competition, Morton, an important frozen food purveyor at the time, introduced a line of frozen donuts into supermarkets throughout the country. These packaged frozen honey-dipped and jelly donuts were all the rage, earning Morton the prize of being the purveyor of the most successful frozen food entry of the decade. Alarm bells went off for me. These frozen treats might displace or—at the very least—put a serious dent into our sale of take-home donuts.

Added to these formidable challenges was the massive escalation of coffee and grain prices in the mid-1970s. The combination of the

Soviet wheat deal of 1972 and the Brazilian coffee frost of 1975 caused those commodities to escalate to highs not seen in 125 years. The price of this market basket of foodstuffs, used to make our products in our stores, soared 40 percent in just one year, causing severe profit issues.

It was against this complex backdrop of challenges that we strategized and laid out our plans for the future.

STRATEGY

Our mission during this era remained very targeted. Nothing fancy here. We wanted to be the dominant retailer of donuts and coffee, achieving at least 50 percent of the coffee and donut shop sales in each of the markets we earmarked for development.

Our objective was to increase earnings per share by at least 20 percent compounded each year and to keep debt no greater than 50 percent of our capitalization.

We focused on five strategic initiatives to achieve our objectives:

1. To double new-store growth from fifty new stores per year to one hundred. You may remember that in 1973, in order to better focus on our core business, we throttled back to forty openings per year. Now that we had a better handle on where and how to grow, we decided to gear up again in an attempt to ensure that our markets were fortressed to withstand the onslaught of expected competition.

2. To gain a better control over our sourcing and make the system less vulnerable to the vagaries of the commodity market. This initiative would enable us to better protect store profitability for our franchise owners.

3. To dramatically increase our advertising investment to be able to fend off our exploding competition.

4. To strategically add complementary new products to the menu to raise same-store sales and store profit.

5. To improve store standards through remodeling and better operations.

Here's how we went about executing each of these five critical initiatives:

1. Double new-store growth.

Accelerating store growth was concerning to most of the board as well as a few members of our team. They all understood that a decade earlier growing too fast was at the root of our rock bottom year and all the pain attendant to that. But we had taken giant steps to strategize the process for new-store development, improving by leaps and bounds on the old days where reliance on my site visits was the sum total of our quality control. Gone were the days of my parachuting into a strange city, being driven to a prospective site, sniffing the air around me, and deciding whether to proceed.

Replacing our old system was a very computer-literate staff. They resided in what I termed "the war room." We had purchased all the demographic data anyone might want about consumers in a community. This included maps of each metropolitan area in the United States showing all competitive locations and ranking each community's desirability for growth, including costs to sustain an advertising campaign. We hired location consultants to run regression analyses in order to measure and quantify each characteristic that made for a successful site. In the end, we were able to rank every major downtown area and thoroughfare in each community from most to least desirable. We knew just how many shops we could open in each city and ranked the best order to develop them.

At the time, *Sales Management* magazine listed about three hundred SMSAs (Statistical Marketing Sales Areas) in the United States. An SMSA was generally an individual TV market. To illustrate, Boston would be considered one SMSA, but it incorporated all the communities that fell within the TV coverage range. That SMSA might cover an area of 4.5 million people ranging from Fall River, Massachusetts, in the south to Salem, New Hampshire, in the north.

We were actively developing shops in about thirty of those SMSAs. Since many were among the largest cities in the United

States, the population in those markets might include up to 50 or
60 percent of the US population.

We were intensifying our focus with respect to new-store development, not so much interested in the number of stores we opened but
where we opened them. We wanted to be the preeminent brand in
our category in each market we elected to compete in. We were firm
believers that our success was significantly more tied to our brand
strength in a market than it was to the number of stores we had
spread throughout the country. We viewed this notion as fortressing
a market. We also believed a well-fortressed market could withstand
and possibly beat back later incursions by competitors. Years later,
this was to prove the case when Tim Hortons, the Canadian donut
chain, attempted to enter New England, one of our most fortressed
strongholds. It wasn't long before they closed those shops.

To build a brand in a market, we needed both a distribution of
stores as well as consistent advertising dollars. In those markets
where we had both, initial opening sales and yearly same-store sales
growth were the highest.

Our analysis found a direct correlation between certain weeks of
advertising and same-store sales gains. Same-store sales were the
critical measurement indicating year-over-year sale gains. Percentage same-store sales gains were healthier in markets where we could
afford to advertise twenty-six weeks at one and a half impressions
per week per viewer (measured in ad talk as 150 gross ratings points
per week) versus markets where we could advertise fewer weeks.

We did even better when we advertised thirty-eight weeks at 150
gross rating points, and better still when we could afford fifty-two
weeks a year. Our goal was to develop 70 percent of our new stores
in developed markets; those were the SMSAs where we could advertise at least twenty-six weeks per year. The remaining 30 percent of
new development was earmarked for markets where we could
achieve that critical mass within three to five years.

The final decision as to the acceptability of a proposed location
still rested on a site visit by the vice president of development. But
now, he was supported by a host of tools including a store sales

projection model that was designed to project sales plus or minus 10 percent, nine out of ten times. Armed with these improved selection tools, I was confident we could safely ramp up new-store development from forty stores per year to a hundred.

2. Gain a better control over our sourcing and make the system less vulnerable to the vagaries of the commodity market.

This initiative would enable us to better protect store profitability for our franchise owners by roping in our product costs. We had just lived through what can only be called a tsunami-size increase in commodity costs due to the Russian wheat deal of 1972 and the Brazilian coffee frost of 1975.

Russia had suffered severe crop shortages in the early 1970s when the US government decided to ship ten million tons of wheat and corn to Russia at subsidized prices. At the time, the press commonly referred to it as the Great Grain Robbery. I might have seen that as a cute play on words, mocking the Great Train Robbery, had it not been for the disastrous implications it had for our business. Within ten months of the shipment, soybeans soared from $3.30 per bushel to $12.90. We fried our donuts in soybean oil. By the time agricultural commodity costs finally peaked in 1974, the commodities we used to make our product had increased by 40 percent.

Only a year later, we were whacked again, this time by the Brazilian coffee frost. In July of 1975, 70 percent of the coffee plants in the best coffee growing regions of Brazil were lost due to a very severe frost. A large percent of our coffee consisted of high-quality beans from this region. The price of Brazilian coffee tripled in that crop season.

It was during this time that our newly hired director of purchasing, Len Geller, conceived and implemented a transformational way to price the manufacture and distribution of our products. Tom Schwarz had hired Len from the McDonald's purchasing department in 1971. Len, in a series of moves over an eight-year period, unbundled each step in the sourcing process in a unique way that ultimately saved the average store approximately 5 percent of its sales. His contribution was one of the critical turning points in the history of the brand. By my calculations, in 1972, the average store was spending 35 percent of each sales dollar on food and paper supplies. By 1980, that number had fallen to 30 percent

Before Len's arrival, we approved certain manufacturers to provide foodstuffs to our stores based on their ability to meet end-product specifications. Each manufacturer had a salesman who received a commission on the sale, and the product was distributed through an approved distributor who made a percentage markup on the products they delivered.

Len's brilliance was in not only conceiving a revolutionary purchasing system that was totally new to the food service industry but in seamlessly engineering its acceptance throughout the system. His vision was to objectively segment each step of the sourcing process and introduce total transparency and maximum efficiency. To begin, he formed a committee of franchise leaders from around the country and shared his plan. He gained their support and began his program in New England. Once proven there, the agreement was to roll it out to the rest of the country.

Since we were barred by antitrust law from requiring our franchise owners to purchase goods from us, Len built on our existing shortening futures program. This was a program whereby franchise owners had agreed to buy all their shortening needs from a designated distributor and we, in turn, advised the distributor based on our readings of the market regarding the best time to buy shortening. By our accounts, this DCP, or Distributor Commitment Program, saved the average store approximately $2,000 per year when we first introduced it.

Len proposed we expand this process to all food and paper supplies. He undertook a forensic study of the costs and processes used by the distributor in supplying our stores. With the advice of his franchise committee, he was able to improve payment and delivery policies, which promised to save the distributor a great deal of money. In exchange, the distributor agreed to change the customary percentage markup universal in the trade to a fixed price of seventy-five cents per carton. The logic was inescapable: if shortening escalated in price from $25 for a fifty-pound cube to $75 because of commodity increases, and the distributor charged a 5 percent markup for delivery, then the delivery costs for that fifty-pound cube shot up from $1.25 to $3.75 without any corresponding cost increase to the distributor. This first step moved all food and paper except for dairy to one delivery per week for all goods and yielded a significant savings to our franchise owners.

The next step once all purchases were centralized through the distributor was to use competitive bidding for each of the important ingredients: coffee, shortening, donut mix, fillings, and paper goods. With the help of Andre Bolaffi, our chief of quality control, we set clear specifications and used timing and leverage to get much better prices. Gone were the salesmen commissions and inefficient supplier deals to garner business. Each region, as this was being rolled out, had a DCP committee that met with Len regularly, oversaw the bidding procedure, and agreed on quantity and winning bids. Franchise-owner support was so strong that Len's suggestions on timing and amounts were generally followed to the letter. We had few if any recommendations not executed by the regional committees.

The next phase was to do a forensic accounting of the manufacturers' processes and come to an agreement on both a fair perpound tolling charge for the use of their plant and equipment, and a negotiation of a fair cost-per-pound for their profit. Once that was done, we could advise the manufacturer as to the best timing to buy individual ingredients. If we used hard or soft wheat in our donut mix along with sugar and eggs, each component had its own market and a best time and amount to buy to ensure we were getting maximum efficiency.

The last step in the transformation was Len's proposal to form a cooperative for the franchisees to own the regional distribution centers. He approached the National Cooperative Bank in Washington for the initial financing to buy the land and the one-acre distribution facility. He planned to have the regional DCP committees hire a center manager who in turn would arrange for the leasing of the trucks and trailers as well as the hiring of the drivers. Each participating franchise had only to put up a $100 initial fee and was entitled to a patronage dividend based upon their usage if and when the centers made a profit. And they always made a profit.

It is impossible to overstate the benefit this purchasing regime had on our system and the success of our brand. The impact of an average store's profitability ramping from 10–12 percent of sales all the way up to 15–17 percent was tremendous.

3. Dramatically increase our advertising investment to be able to fend off our exploding competition.

Another major innovation that shaped the last five years of the 1970s and transformed the brand occurred in marketing. These changes were ably led by Sid Feltenstein, senior vice president of marketing. In this role, Sid engineered and managed not only a transformation of the brand but our method of marketing it. He accomplished this with three major initiatives.

The first was already in motion when Sid arrived at his marketing post. As the store profits began to blossom due to the purchasing changes Len Geller was implementing, our franchise owners in Providence, rather than pocketing all the increased profits, decided to double their advertising spend in the market. Sales responded immediately and the market began to outperform the average sales increase experienced in the rest of the country. It didn't take long for this phenomenon to reach senior management. We discussed this at our national advisory council meeting and rather quickly reached the conclusion that we should try this nationally.

The franchise-owner leadership was hesitant to quickly change contracts from a 2 percent advertising spend, in accordance with our existing contracts, to a 4 percent spend in perpetuity. But we agreed to try it for an eighteen-month trial and, if successful, consider a permanent change. The leadership was concerned about free riders, so we made the threshold an 80 percent participation rate before putting it into effect. I'm a little cloudy on the exact percentage of participation, but my guess is that almost 90 percent of the system agreed to the trial.

And off we went: increasing our media spend from $2.7 million in 1977 to $6 million in 1978, showcasing the brand on prime-time shows and in prime spots. We advertised on *The Tonight Show* regularly and Johnny Carson sent a signed picture of himself to each franchise owner telling them how glad he was that they were a part of his advertising family. Average sales per store that year were up 7.5 percent. We were all proud and thrilled that everyone all over the country was getting to know us.

On the basis of our results, we thought a permanent change to 4 percent after the eighteen-month trial was a mere formality. That was not to be the case. When the time came to re-up, a significant number of franchise owners were hesitant. When the extra advertising stopped, sales began to soften a bit. It was at this point that our national advisory chairmen helped us draft a new offer to the system. This amendment to our franchise agreements increased advertising spend from 2 to 4 percent permanently. We also sweetened the deal by extending our standard twenty-year franchise agreement by an additional ten years, agreeing to keep the financial terms the same for the extension period. This longer time period with known contract provisions was a significant benefit to the franchisees.

In exchange for the longer contract period, we negotiated a majority clause that stipulated if 60 percent or more stores in a market agreed to an even higher ad spend, then everyone in the market was bound. We finally had our deal and could now build the brand in a serious way. This change had many significant benefits.

We finally had a much larger and more prestigious national megaphone to communicate with our consumers. The added prestige of national advertising also helped increase the resale value of existing stores, and now the company could begin to move into a broader array of markets aided by these TV buys.

Simultaneously, Sid had begun to direct our new ad agency, New York–based Ally and Gargano, to create a memorable advertising campaign. He reasoned that with most of our sales not yet in coffee but in donuts, supermarkets were our prime competitor. To capitalize on our superior product, the agency created the iconic campaign "Time to Make the Donuts," which highlighted all the efforts we went through to create a superior product.

In this campaign, Michael Vale, a character actor with a memorable demeanor, became the loveable "Fred the Baker." Fred was featured in commercial after commercial trudging off to make the donuts, spouting quips like, "I bet supermarkets don't do this." While fun and lighthearted, this was hard-hitting advertising, as well as an unmitigated hit with consumers. People all over the country began describing their trek to their jobs—or any difficult work— with "It's time to make the donuts." The campaign lasted seventeen years and won three Clios, the advertising equivalent to the Academy Awards.

The second major innovation Sid implemented had to do with how we organized our marketing department. In retailing, the rule of thumb is to keep the "news" coming—create a continual stream of new and enticing offers for the consumer. The "news" could be new products, price-off promotions, premiums, or the opportunity to win prizes. To accomplish this, Sid organized the marketing department in the model of a consumer packaged goods company.

After college, Sid began his career at Procter and Gamble, and he had not forgotten how they were organized. He began by establishing a product management department; at the helm he installed Glenn Bacheller, a bright young executive from Gorton's, a division of General Mills. Sid assigned all our products into one of three categories: beverages, donuts, or bakery.

This organizational format is now pretty standard at most large fast feeders, but it was cutting edge as the 1970s drew to a close. It was the job of each category leader to manage the progress of the products under their control. He or she would measure their products versus the competition for quality and price. They would also be responsible for product extensions and new product offerings in their category. All new product ideas would be ballot-tested with consumers; all promising ideas would be turned over to R&D to develop prototypes. Ideas from all three product managers would compete against each other for testing and rollout. We might have six new products or product extensions rolled out per year, and the ones that seemed most promising and capable of delivering the greatest profit would make it to field test. This organizational change really boosted innovation in all product categories.

The first product manager in charge of beverages was a standout. Kim Lopdrup had come to us from Procter and Gamble where he had been a product manager for Folgers Coffee and Citrus Hill orange juice. Kim immediately helped our coffee business by introducing Dunkin' Decaf. He pioneered coffee by-the-pound for take-home use, improved sip-through lids on coffee-to-go cups, iced coffee, and a larger coffee-to-go size. He was also instrumental in our going forward with advertising coffee on TV.

On the basis of Kim's success as product manager, Sid promoted him to vice president of advertising, merchandising, and sales promotion. There he oversaw the "Fred the Baker" campaign, creating memorable ads that widely outscored the industry norms. Finally, Sid appointed Irv Eison vice president of research and development. We now had in place a first-rate marketing organization.

4. Strategically add complementary new products to the menu to raise same-store sales and profits.

Another big idea Sid championed was the creation of a bakery category. Up until he instituted the product management system, innovation was pretty much a hit-or-miss affair. Ideas might come from franchise owners or operational personnel. Now all ideas were funneled through the product managers, and if none were forthcoming from elsewhere you could rest assured they would have a plate full to suggest if for no other reason than to justify their existence.

Sid saw huge potential in installing an oven in our stores to supplement our fried donut line with a wide range of baked goods. He insisted that "the oven is the big new product this year, not the product we are going to bake in it. That's only the beginning." This was a big move for us. It required a major investment in equipment and the teaching of new production skills to our personnel. It also required us to remerchandise our scarce shelf space to accommodate baked goods. Irv Eisen, now head of R&D, began to work on developing a line of top-notch baked goods. He started out simply with just two kinds of muffins, blueberry and corn.

I traditionally relied on the technical skill of our research and development team to develop new products, but when it came to our first baked product—blueberry muffins—I made an exception. Like many Bostonians, I had a vivid memory of the delicious muffins sold at one of our two iconic department store chains, Jordan Marsh (Filenes being the other). On their top-floor dining area, the store baked and sold large muffins crowned with a sugary top and stuffed with blueberries. These muffins were well known and much loved throughout New England.

I insisted we try to replicate the Jordan Marsh blueberry muffin, but try as we might, we were never able to obtain the exact recipe. Through trial and error, we came close. Turned out that in addition to a mix rich in eggs, butter, and all-purpose flour, the secret to a great blueberry muffin was a generous portion of wild blueberries.

Wild, lowbush blueberries are grown only in Atlantic Canada and Maine. These berries have significantly more flavor than cultivated blueberries, their high-bush cousins. *That* was our secret. We would select only the best wild blueberries after fall harvest and flash freeze them for availability all year long. Wild blueberries contain less moisture than cultivated berries and keep their shape through the mixing process. We next experimented with what I called fruit-to-crumb ratios, tinkering endlessly in pursuit of the perfect balance. To the best of my memory, the winning number was 15 to 20 percent wild blueberries in the mix. We finished them off with a sweet, crunchy sugar topping.

Once we had an oven in each shop, Irv and his team followed up with a line of high-quality cookies. In subsequent years, we introduced croissants, and in the 1990s, bagels. These innovative baked goods along with beverage and other promotional "news" kept our same-store sales growing for decades.

5. Improve store standards with remodeling.

The last strategic initiative was a new logo and store design in a push to upgrade operational standards. Our raspberry, pink, and white design had served us since the 1960s but was beginning to look tired and dated. We hired noted architect and designer Charlie Moore to design the new store and Sandgren and Murtha to update our logo. Both came out smashingly well. Moore changed the color palette to earthen tones of light brown and touches of orange, while Sandgren and Murtha used the plump Frankfurter typeface to develop the luscious orange and raspberry logo still in use today. As soon as we remodeled our stores, sales jumped on average by 20 percent. Not only did the customers respond favorably to these updates and, in my opinion, better design, the store staff did as well. Refreshing their environment seemed to raise their game: they delivered better service and kept their new digs spic and span, making recruitment easier as well.

From 1978 through 1983, our five interrelated strategies worked wonderfully. We effectively fortressed a number of markets, keeping Tim Hortons and Winchell's from expanding into our own. Our heavy investment in network TV, the superior profits reaped from our revolutionary purchasing system, and our new store design all added up to make our franchise so much more desirable than our donut competitors. We emerged from this era as the unquestionable leader in our field.

In the ten years that followed the dark days of our loss in 1973, we posted forty consecutive quarters of increased earnings, with sales growing by 300 percent and profits by 700 percent. We had nearly thirteen hundred stores open and $100 million in assets.[3]

ORGANIZATION

The centralized organization we had created in 1973 was working well. My primary job during this period was to recruit and retain great people. I said as much in Donald Clifford and Richard Cavanagh's 1985 book, *The Winning Performance: How America's High-Growth Midsize Companies Succeed.* When asked what my primary responsibility was during this period, I responded: "My number one job is to create an environment where good people can work."[4]

Of course, having the right strategy was as crucial as having the right people in the right jobs; having a sensible and generous compensation plan was also critical. Tom and I worked hard on this and continually reviewed it to make sure it was working.

We compensated our senior managers in three ways. First was to pay annual base salaries in at least the middle of the range for comparable jobs industry wide. That portion of the compensation package generally amounted to a third of the compensation. Next was an annual bonus paid in proportion to the achievement of the company's agreed-upon goals at the beginning of the fiscal year, another third of the compensation package. The last third was based on long-term compensation (LTI).

These long-term payouts were based on how well we performed against our budgeted objectives three years in the future. This was to ensure that management balanced decisions and actions that considered both short- and long-term implications. In effect, this LTI safeguarded against management taking shortsighted actions that focused on protecting or maximizing annual bonuses at the expense of longer-term performance.

This three-part compensation program placed two-thirds of a senior manager's compensation at risk since it was dependent on performance. In that way, the senior managers' interests were directly in line with the company's stockholders. These long-term incentives were paid in cash or stock. In a growing company, I have found that stock options (or in a private company, phantom stock) are a wonderful approach to attract and retain top talent. It's one of the best ways to help a company punch way above its weight in terms of performance. Many talented managers are attracted to companies that offer the opportunity to not only earn a decent salary but to amass real wealth.

We reserved 10 percent of the shares outstanding for option grants, which were ten-year grants with five-year vesting. This meant the price of the shares was set at the time of the grant. The executive received one-fifth of the amount each year but had ten years' worth of earnings growth before the option had to be exercised.

These grants also served as a golden handcuff. Any executive who wished to leave before his fifth or tenth anniversary would be relinquishing a sizable benefit. I was not a big believer in granting options to middle managers and below. I felt it diluted the amount I had for the top twenty or so decision-makers that most formed and impacted strategy. The marketplace for top talent is highly competitive and headhunters know where the talent is. I found the most important element in recruiting and retaining talent is the right work environment, but after that, it is total compensation.

Lower-level managers were paid a smaller percentage of their base in annual incentives and more in base salary. Their annual bonuses were geared more toward their own budgeted achievements, as opposed to overall corporate results. We believed they had less impact over the annual corporate results and could less afford to have a high percentage of their salary at risk.

For all employees, especially for nonexempt, hourly employees who (by law) are paid for overtime, we calculated and annually shared an individual wealth plan. The plan detailed where each employee stood against our objective of having every twenty-year employee able to retire at 66 percent of their average salary for the last three years of their employment. We had a very generous 401(k) plan that increased company matching contributions as years of service increased.

Our compensation system spoke loudly about our beliefs and values. We wanted people to receive fair compensation while they worked and to be heavily motivated to achieve budgeted results. We also wanted our people to stay for an entire career. If they did, they would be able to retire in dignity and not suffer a massive change in living standards. For senior managers, we did this through our stock option program, and for other levels of management and nonexempt employees we achieved this through our 401(k).

Our turnover was quite low—just 10 percent a year—which was about half the national average. And of that number, most was involuntary (firings for substandard performance). In addition, our top fifteen executives had served in the company an average of fifteen years, a record for which we were very proud. Clearly, we understood the benefit of bringing in new talent to teach us new things and help us grow, but we were also very much believers in continuity as a key lever to growth.

COMMUNICATION

A key component of my communications responsibility began with our internal operating committee. This committee met monthly and comprised the top six executives in the company: me; Tom Schwarz; Ralph Gabellieri, head of operations; Sid Feltenstein, head of marketing; Jim Dangelo, head of development (real estate and franchising); and Larry Hantman, general counsel. Other senior managers might be invited, depending on the agenda.

I drafted each meeting's agenda but made sure I asked other attendees for suggested topics as well. During at least two meetings per year we would revisit our simulated model and the assumptions we were using to do our short- and long-range planning. We would often debrief one another on the insights and discoveries gleaned from the hundred or so store visits each of us took during the year, using this feedback to measure the mood of our franchisees, to see how well our programs were working, and to make any adjustments to the plan that might be needed.

We also used these meetings to prepare for our quarterly advisory council meeting. Each quarter, senior management met with the chairmen and vice chairmen of each of our five zone advisory boards. This is when we reviewed how store profitability was faring against our objectives and whether our strategic initiatives were achieving those objectives. It was also an opportunity to hear from management and franchise owners tasked with analyzing and recommending changes on important system issues such as the design for the store of the future or a program to increase advertising investment.

One important operating committee meeting each year dealt with the annual budget call. Our fiscal year ended on the last Saturday in October. To budget for the new fiscal year, I would send out a budget call in writing to the entire organization sometime in late spring. Before I issued the call, the operating committee would review and agree on the major elements of what I was going to say—guidelines on same-store sales, new-store development, major R&D projects, and company store margins.

I would emphasize our mission and objectives as well as five or six company-wide initiatives, stressing in my call that each store, district, and region was unique: *I was not sending out a prescription but rather a guideline.* I was a big believer in a budgetary process that had real input and commitment from everyone in the organization. Most everyone was a profit or at least a cost center, and all had some portion of their compensation dependent on how well they did against the objectives they set. We clearly needed their buy-in.

Budget reviews took place during the summer. All heads of a profit or cost center throughout the company would review their budget for the coming year in person with their respective supervisors. The process called for each department to assess the risks inherent in their budget and to assess a probability of the risk actually occurring. We also asked for a contingency plan that might be used to offset slippage.

I strongly believed there should only be one budget. I was aware that in some companies, a "stretch" budget is encouraged by senior management, while they in turn submit a lesser number to their board. The theory here is that the team will put in more effort if they have a stretch number to hit. In our case, my team set a very aggressive budget to begin with—if anything, I had to temper it. We stuck with this one budget and didn't modify it as the year progressed, though we did highlight for the board the risks (and probabilities) inherent in the plan as well as our contingency options. I thought this alignment important: we were all singing off the same song sheet.

Each year in late August or early September, we invited management to a three-day meeting in Boston. We'd rent a big hall, getting things rolling late on a Sunday afternoon. The first event was a state of the company address, something that I spent a great deal of time and effort drafting. I used this speech to remind the team of the significance of our work. Yes, it was donuts and coffee—I understood that—but we all knew it was about more than that. I drew the picture of millions of people starting their day with us: our delicious coffee and fresh bakery products putting a smile on their faces and a skip in their step. I believed and contended the world was a better place because of us. Millions of people depended on us for a happier start to their day.

I also reminded those in the audience of the difference we made in the lives of hundreds of franchisees and their families, potentially impacting thousands and thousands of lives. We provided a business system that enabled all these families to achieve their dreams, something that may not have happened if it wasn't for the work we did.

In my state-of-the-company address I would also lay out the challenges and opportunities we faced, along with the mission, objectives, and key strategies we were employing. I always gave a realistic assessment, yet at the same time I wrapped it in a healthy dose of optimism about our abilities to achieve our goals.

At the conclusion of the talk, we'd break for cocktails followed by a nice dinner. The after-dinner portion of the program was what I looked forward to the most each year. It was then that we celebrated teammates as they reached important career landmarks: five-, ten-, fifteen-, and twenty-year anniversaries. These were part roast, part serious reviews of the important achievements the teammates contributed and their impact on the company. Here, too, a group of us worked hard on each acknowledgment. I often relied on Neil Guanci, a longtime operations vice president and natural comic. I also turned to Tom. He was blessed with an incredible wit. On a few occasions, I even hired a comedy writer to help make the event as memorable as possible.

At this dinner, we'd select someone who'd made a particularly major contribution during the year to receive the William Rosenberg Innovation Award. My father presented the winner with the trophy.

The following day, a Monday, we might rent a country club for the day, take a cruise to the Boston Harbor Islands, or—in the early days—travel to my father's horse farm in New Hampshire. The idea was to have fun and get to know one another in an informal setting. Teammates could play golf, tennis, softball, or swim. As part of the festivities, we had an annual cookout.

Tuesday, the final day, we featured speeches by other members of senior management. One of the most anticipated highlights was the presentation of the marketing calendar for the coming year, along with the new commercials. Usually, the marketing department was supported by live talent and would wow us with a full singing and dancing revue. I think these meetings conveyed beautifully the respect and admiration we had for our team. And in return I believe most participants, if not all, left these meetings informed and energized to face the new fiscal year.

CRISIS MANAGEMENT

This era of the company's history was free from the life-or-death issues that required so much of my attention in the earlier days. We were the clear winner in our category and had begun to refine our management processes to get our business under control.

Although I encouraged each senior manager to join outside trade associations to help us track what was going on in the world, that task continued to be an important role for me as well. Though I retired from the International Franchise Association board, relinquishing my seat to our general counsel, Larry Hantman, I joined the National Restaurant Association board to ensure we were learning as much about restaurant industry issues as we had about franchising matters through our IFA membership.

I had not replaced CFO Bill Beebe, who resigned in 1973. I was blessed with three able department chiefs in this area, who now reported to me: Dick Hart as treasurer; Tom Burger, in charge of information technology; and Bernie Patriacca, VP and controller.

We had no investor relations or financial public relations firm. Investor relations were generally handled by Dick Hart, our treasurer. Tom and I would hold one or two luncheons a year in Boston and New York for investors or analysts who were interested in our company. I would speak at the annual analysts' meetings held throughout the year by various brokerage houses when invited to participate.

Occasionally, an analyst would call and request a meeting. One such call came in 1978, and I welcomed him to our offices for a chat.

He was a youngish man with a shock of white hair. He introduced himself as Peter Lynch, representing the Magellan Fund. I had no idea what the Magellan Fund was or anything about Peter. Our company's stock had plummeted from the go-go days of 1969 when we were a high flyer. Sure, we had gotten our arms around the business and had been showing impressive profit growth since our loss in 1973, but Wall Street has a very long memory, and there wasn't a lot of interest in our stock at the time.

I spent what I remember was an enjoyable hour or so with Lynch explaining the business and our plans. A few months later, I was watching *Wall $treet Week with Louis Rukeyser*. This was in the days before CNBC, Bloomberg, and Fox Business Channel. PBS had *Nightly Business Report* each night, and the big kahuna was the Rukeyser show on Friday nights at eight. I tried to watch it religiously. And there on the Rukeyser show, sitting on the couch being interviewed by Louis, was this guy with the shock of white hair. Louis announced that Peter Lynch was the most successful mutual fund manager in the country, and his Magellan Fund for Fidelity had billions of dollars under management.

To my astonishment, Peter began telling the financial world all about his best pick: Dunkin' Donuts! I was stunned and elated. I literally danced to the phone and excitedly called Tom and Larry: "You've got to turn on the TV. We are being featured on PBS as the hottest thing since sliced bread!"

From that moment on, our stock started to climb. Peter and Magellan became our largest stockholder. They owned as much as 15–20 percent of our stock. Peter went on to write some bestsellers about his days at Magellan. One of his books, *One Up on Wall Street*, talks about Dunkin' Donuts as one of his great "ten baggers," meaning he made ten times his investment for his mutual fund holders investing in our stock.[5]

LESSON EIGHT:
The Exceptional Benefits of Franchising

Franchising is a method for expanding a business and distributing goods and services through a licensing relationship. A franchisor gives the rights to conduct business under its trademarks. Franchisors specify the products and services that will be offered, provide an operating system, brand, and support. The franchisee is the person or company granted the right to do business under the franchisor's trademark. In exchange, the franchisee pays fees to the franchisor.

The roots of franchising go back to the mid-nineteenth century. It began with German brewers licensing local taverns to buy and advertise their beer. In the 1920s, Howard Johnson utilized this system to dot the highways and byways of America with orange-topped Ho-Jo restaurants. Franchisees would buy their ice cream and foodstuffs from Howard Johnson commissaries.

The real explosive growth of franchising came after the end of WWII. The creation of the interstate highway system in the 1950s transformed America, giving rise to the automobile culture and suburbia. Before the war, only one out of three women worked outside the home; after the war, that number began to rise to two out of three. Those sea changes in how people worked and lived placed a premium on known brands that delivered value and convenience.

Into this new era, a group of entrepreneurs stepped onto the stage to build new businesses and brands that utilized the franchise system. Ray Kroc, a milkshake machine salesman, saw growth opportunities in a new way to provide tasty sandwiches quickly and inexpensively. Kemmons Wilson was a modest homebuilder who thought he and his fellow homebuilders could use their experience to build a few roadside motels. He named them Holiday Inn, after a Bing Crosby movie. With only a modest pension, sixty-five-year-old "Colonel" Sanders traveled in his Model T Ford from restaurant to restaurant peddling, at "a nickel a head," his recipe for delicious fried chicken.

A brand owner has many options to expand his or her business. He or she may elect to open all future units as company owned, fi-

The Rosenbergs and the Winokurs before the donut wars. (Left to right) Rosenberg's father, Rosenberg, his mother, his sister Carol, his aunt Etta Winokur, his cousin Barbara (later to marry David Slater, Rosenberg's arch competitor in the donut wars), and his uncle Harry Winokur.

Robert Rosenberg

Robt. Rosenberg New Head of Universal Food

Universal Food Systems, Inc. announces the election of Robert Rosenberg, formerly of Waltham, as president. William Rosenberg of Newton, former president and company founder, was named board chairman.

Robert Rosenberg had lived at 1105 Lexington St. until moving recently to Mattapan. William Rosenberg lives at 99 Littlefield Rd.

Under the control of the new president will be UFS' operations of franchised shops of Dunkin' Donuts of America, Industrial Cafeterias, Menu-Mat vending machine services and other subsidiaries grossing $20 million annually.

All of these companies were established by William Rosenberg, who launched his business career with one industrial catering truck in 1946 and expanded the firm into a national, multi-million dollar operation.

Robert Rosenberg, the new president, is a graduate of the Harvard Graduate School of Business Administration and Cornell's Hotel and Restaurant School.

The announcement of Rosenberg's appointment as president of Universal Food Systems in the Waltham News-Tribune, August 30, 1963.

Rosenberg (by the blackboard) with his team at the long table referred to as his "desk" in the early years of Universal Food Systems.

REGENT THEATRE, NORFOLK DOWNS, MASS.

During the early years, Dunkin' Donuts was headquartered on the second floor of this old converted theater in North Quincy, Massachusetts (then known as Norfolk Downs).

Dunkin' Donuts's first TV commercial, circa 1964, featuring actual franchise owners. In the commercial, the owners took a pledge that they would make their donuts fresh every four hours, that they would serve fresh coffee every eighteen minutes, and that their cream would never be milk.

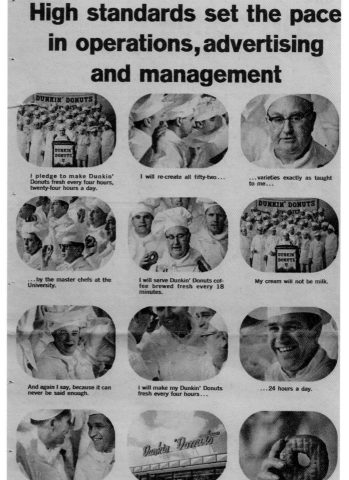

High standards set the pace in operations, advertising and management

I pledge to make Dunkin' Donuts fresh every four hours, twenty-four hours a day.

I will re-create all fifty-two...

...varieties exactly as taught to me...

...by the master chefs at the University.

I will serve Dunkin' Donuts coffee brewed fresh every 18 minutes.

My cream will not be milk.

And again I say, because it can never be said enough.

I will make my Dunkin' Donuts fresh every four hours...

...24 hours a day.

Congratulations graduates. It is now...

up to you, to rise to the greatness of Dunkin' Donuts...

the world's largest chain of coffee and doughnut shops.

Vintage 1950s Dunkin' Donuts porcelain cup and donut box. Both featured the once-omnipresent "Dunkie," the company mascot made from donuts. Rosenberg retired "Dunkie" a few years into his presidency.

Typical early Dunkin' Donuts store design fashioned after architect Bernard Healy's "fishbowl" California-style design.

Dunkin' Donuts Makes Big S-P-L-A-S-H

In British

and West German Newspapers

Clippings from the European press in 1964, featuring Rosenberg's father. The press releases committed Dunkin' Donuts to premature overseas development.

Groundbreaking of the new Dunkin' Donuts headquarters circa 1971. Holding the shovels are board members (left to right) Richard "Archie" Southgate, Homer Severign, Milt Brown, and Robert Rosenberg.

*Opening the Dunkin'
Donuts University
and warehouse in the
Philippines, 1983. The trip
Rosenberg took to Manila
led to a change in how
Dunkin' Donuts went to
market.*

*The Niglios and the Rosenbergs taking a
sightseeing break on the island of Kauai
during an International Franchise Association
Convention, circa early 1980s. Dick Niglio
was the CEO of Mister Donut. (Left to right)
Dick Niglio, Sandy Niglio, Lorna Rosenberg,
and Robert Rosenberg.*

*The Dunkin' Donuts's senior
management team in 1988 at
a surprise party for Rosenberg's
twenty-fifth anniversary as
CEO. (Left to right) Ralph
Gabellieri, Larry Hantman,
Sid Feltenstein, Robert
Rosenberg, Tom Schwarz, Jack
Shafer, and Len Geller.*

A donut baker flips the fresh cut rings to the screen. Just one step in the dance of the donuts!

Edna and Bob Demery, franchise owners and the inventors of Munchkins, with their team.

A Dunkin' Donuts location showcasing the old question mark counter and stools. This setup served as Dunkin' Donuts's service delivery system until the 1980s.

A Dunkin' Donuts location after the removal of the question mark counter, which was replaced with a self-service counter and remote seating.

nancing them with his or her own capital and manning them with his or her own employees. Or, they may select a hybrid system of ownership, with capital provided by the company, and significant profit sharing with local management, creating a virtual franchise. Chick Fil-A has utilized such a system effectively.

Though these options were available, when most of these brand owners faced the decision on how to expand, they overwhelmingly chose the franchise system. This marriage between the brand owner (the franchisor) and the local entrepreneur (franchisee) executing the business in his or her local community brought great benefits to many segments of society.

For the franchisor, licensing to an independent person who has significant "skin in the game" often ensures the business and trademark are distributed in the market with higher and more consistent standards. The franchisor also receives capital from initial fees and often real estate, which can speed growth. The franchisee, who is closer to the customer and competitors, will often suggest adjustments to improve the business.

The franchisee also receives great benefits from this marriage as well. Since the franchisor has an established business and has hopefully perfected many of the operational issues, the purchase of a franchise can dramatically reduce the risk of failure for the aspiring entrepreneur. The pooling of advertising money also greatly increases the advertising might of the business. For example, a single store doing $500,000 a year in sales and spending 4 percent on advertising has a budget of $20,000 per year to reach consumers, whereas a system of five hundred units has a megaphone of $10,000,000 a year to inform customers of new offers. The same can be true in purchasing. A large system can utilize size and professionalism to buy goods at lower prices, ensuring added profits over independents in the same business. Finally, when an entrepreneur decides to sell his business, there is a pool of qualified franchisees already in the system who may buy.

The consumer also benefits from the growth of these franchised outlets. Although there may be some consumers who long for their old local diner, dry cleaner, barroom pizza maker, or nearby tax

preparer, these small businesses are increasingly passing from the scene. The new brands with their array of products, service delivery systems, loyalty programs, and prices are hard to resist. Consumers vote with their feet. Nostalgia aside, when a better deal comes along, customers show up.

Society in general also benefits greatly from this franchise system. Because of the ubiquity of these franchise brands, the general public looks upon these brands as big business. The truth is more nuanced. They are, in fact, enterprises made up of lots of small to midsized firms operating as franchisees. Today there are 750,000 franchise establishments in the United States that employ an estimated eighteen million people and contribute more than $2 trillion a year to the US economy.

As our successful US brands grow globally, franchising is increasingly migrating to other economies around the world. You can imagine what benefit a system that successfully promotes small business ownership can have on employment and social structuring in economies not familiar with capitalism.

Despite all the forgoing benefits of franchising, not all franchise offerings are the same. Some concepts are stronger and provide better odds of success than others. That being the case, how does the prospective franchisor and franchisee decide which franchise is a promising bet?

To both parties I would propose one test to answer this question. The most important metric in determining the strength of a concept is its underlying unit economics, which is measured by calculating the return on investment for an average unit. The ROI is calculated by computing the resultant cash flow of that unit—unaffected by financing considerations—divided by the amount of capital needed to open that unit.[6]

Because margins vary from business to business, I value this ROI test over other popular measurements, such as sales to capital ratios. I prefer a calculation based on first year's sales and resultant cash flow over the use of a discounted cash flow, or DCF model. The DCF model requires future sales and expense projections to obtain a time-valued return. In my opinion, it's too difficult to accurately

project future sales and expense outcomes. I prefer to rely on the proposition that a business will price to protect margins over time, making the initial ROI a more reliable outcome over the life of the unit than the DCF.

It stands to reason that for both the prospective franchisor and franchisee, the higher the ROI the better. In my day, I strove for a 15 percent ROI. Acceptable returns for a franchise offer may vary over time. For example, acceptable returns on a franchise opportunity may be lower today, as returns from other potential competitive investments may also be lower, given current interest rates.

For the would-be franchisor, operating a system with a low ROI runs a real risk of failure. As a system expands, unit sales result in a bell-shaped curve. One-third of the units will achieve above average volume, one-third will reach average volume, and one-third will fall below. If the ROI of an average unit isn't at a healthy rate at the start, it is more than likely the tail (the third ranked below average) will become a real drag on the system. Low returns will create a large inventory of marginal and failed franchisees. As failure mounts, the chain will be unable to attract new owners. Growth is curtailed and the failure of the entire chain is possible.

The tale of Boston Market well illustrates this last point. Years ago, Boston Market had a lot of promise and was a Wall Street darling. The management team was highly regarded for turning Blockbuster Video into a retail giant. This sophisticated team acknowledged Boston Market's low ROIs, but Wall Street—as well as many sophisticated franchisees (many of whom had built successful retail restaurant networks with other brands)—was convinced they could fix the ROI issue over time. Their plan was to build returns through extensive menu additions and to ramp up advertising. This proved dicier than expected. In fact, it was a little like changing the tires on a race car hurtling along the track during the Indianapolis 500. They couldn't pull it off. It wasn't long before the day of reckoning came, wiping out scores of franchisee owners and sinking the stock price to near zero.

A similar fate awaits a prospective franchisee who invests in a concept with a very low ROI. Unless he or she is one of the lucky ones whose unit achieves higher than average annual sales, they are most likely to be disappointed. This very notion was at the heart of the question I posed to every franchisee at each of the one hundred stores I visited yearly: "If you had to invest in this franchise all over again, knowing what you know now, would you do it?" Some franchisees were quite sophisticated, comparing ROIs before making a decision to buy; others did not. But I believe those who did not calculate the world that way had an intuitive sense as to whether returns for their effort and risk were worth it. Their answers were extraordinarily valuable in helping us understand whether or not we were doing our job.

MERRILY WE ROLL ALONG, UNTIL WE DON'T

BACKGROUND

In 1983, after ten years of executing the same strategy, it was clear our world was changing—and in a big way. All signs pointed to the fact that we were going to have to change as well if we were to continue to achieve our objectives.

Same-store sales growth was slowing—slashed in half from its historic 6 percent to now approximately 3 percent. The customer had a new face; the competition had morphed.

A strong demographic trend that had been fueling the growth of the quick-service food industry had begun to slow: the rate at which women were entering the workforce. In the preceding thirty-five years, that number had doubled from one of three women to two of three. But that trend had slowed to a crawl. Most women who could work or needed to had already entered the workforce.

In addition, the baby boomers—the largest consumer cohort in the country up to that time—were aging. This demographic had begun to prefer a more elaborate dining experience than self-service fast food. In the 1980s, new chains that featured table service and somewhat more expensive and exotic offerings began to pop up everywhere. Chili's, Friday's, and Applebee's fit in a new category called casual dining. No question—some of the dining-away-from-home dollars were being siphoned off by this new type of competitor.

We also were coming up against some hard facts about limitations in our own concept. True, we enjoyed great success when we were first to market. But we were learning that habit was a strong predictor for what people chose for their morning pick-me-up. Despite our significant quality advantages, customers around the country demonstrated a reluctance to change from a product choice and taste they grew up with. We were discovering that ingrained habits took time and money to change. As we moved westward to new markets, we engaged in hand-to-hand combat to wean customers away from the 7-Elevens and other convenience store chains that now enjoyed the lion's share of the away-from-home beverage business. Our sales and profits began to suffer with this expansion. The fact was, if our concept couldn't generate a healthy return on investment in these markets, we couldn't safely grow. Commensurately, if we were trapped in our existing successful regions, we worried we ultimately would run out of room to expand.

Our simulated model showed a continual slowing in future earnings growth as we ran our same-store sales and new-store growth assumptions shaped by these emerging realities. Clearly it was time to innovate—and not in a minor way. As this new era in our history dawned, we began to implement four major initiatives to stimulate future growth. We had no idea at the time which of these ideas would bear fruit. As it turned out, two worked beyond our fondest expectations; one was a modest contributor; and the fourth, the initiative furthest from our core business, seems to have been unnecessary and possibly a bridge too far.

STRATEGY

Our strategic initiatives remained the same, but the scope of where and how we developed new locations changed dramatically.

1. International Expansion

In the early 1980s, we decided to put our international expansion into high gear. We created an international department and began to license entire countries to qualified buyers; these were existing large retail companies, such as Seibu in Japan, or well-financed and successful businesspeople from Colombia, the Philippines, England, Hong Kong, Indonesia, and Thailand.

We did not follow an intentional plan but rather sold a country under a negotiated development agreement to buyers who approached us. In those days, everything "American," particularly our fast food and certain movies, were among our country's most successful exports. A number of international investors knocked on our door seeking the rights to develop the Dunkin' Donuts brand in their respective countries.

Our standard agreement with international licensees provided for an up-front franchise fee of several hundred thousand dollars along with a commitment to build new stores each year to retain exclusivity. After an agreed number of openings, the investor "owned" the right to the territory in perpetuity, subject to the stipulation that the agreement could be terminated for cause. Since the country licensee was expected to provide the majority of day-to-day supervision, these international agreements often called for a reduced ongoing royalty compared to the fee paid in the US.

International development was not a get-rich-quick scheme. Setting up a new country required a good deal of up-front investment on our part. Costs included negotiating the deal, legal costs to memorialize it, sourcing foodstuffs in the licensed country, finalizing location approvals, and putting together shop-opening crews. Even our hefty one-time up-front fees barely covered our costs. Establishing operations in any new country took as much as a decade and a hundred stores before it provided meaningful income to us.

It was becoming quite clear that this kind of geographic expansion could prove as difficult as full business diversification. Each country had different beverage habits. Each had its own unique eating patterns when it came to breakfast and snacking. Our concept had to be adapted in each market—most stores sold primarily donuts and baked goods, not beverages. And when beverages were popular, they often were fruit juice drinks, not American coffee.

It was also proving difficult to pick the investors who had the right stuff to develop the brand in each market. We were failing in one-third of the countries, modestly successful in another third, and flourishing in the last. Unfortunately, where we were doing well and enough stores had opened where control of the market had passed exclusively to the country franchise holder, the franchisees often negotiated for lower ongoing royalties.

In less successful markets where exclusivity had not been reached, I quickly learned that judicial views on contracts in other countries were for the most part vastly different from the US. In Japan, the goal was to turn our contract into a nonexclusive with Seibu, because they failed to live up to their development agreement. Exclusivity for them was agreed at fifty stores and they stopped growing at thirty-five. Seibu was one of Japan's largest retail conglomerates; they owned the Seibu department stores, thousands of convenience stores, and the worldwide Intercontinental Hotel chain. On paper, they seemed to be the perfect partner for development in Japan. In reality, that was not the case: the Mister Donut licensee in Japan was beating us in that market, despite starting up at the same time. They had opened several hundred locations in contrast to our measly thirty-five. I was set on finding another partner in Japan to help us combat our competitor, but the courts were slow and seemingly unsympathetic to our plight.

I was fit to be tied. And it wasn't just me—the entire team hated to lose. Here we were, watching this hundred-million-person market slip through our fingers, and I was powerless to do anything about it. I ultimately had to stop the suit, kiss and make up with my licensee, and just watch as Mister Donut virtually put us out of business in Japan. Duskin Company, the Mister Donut licensee, forced International Multifoods, Mister Donut's worldwide parent company, to sell them the rights not only to Japan but future development rights for the Mister Donut concept throughout Asia. A big cost and a big lesson. My lesson here was that in international business the courts are far more sympathetic to the home team than to any outsider. I also came away with the understanding that when you sell rights to your franchise in a country, you are in effect giving up control of your brand in that country.

Although international expansion had to be a part of our future if we wanted brand leadership, it did not appear to be a solution to our earnings gap in the short term. It was clear to me we still had a lot to learn about adapting our concept from country to country and where and how to market our concept internationally.

2. Reconfiguring the Standard Shop and Delivery System

Fortunately, the next two initiatives did not suffer from the same limitations as overseas expansion. Quite the contrary: a change in our thinking about where and how we sold our products in the US and a reconfiguration of our shops had a speedy and transformational impact on our fortunes.

The early 1980s found us in the process of remodeling the chain using new colors and a fresh logo. In addition, two franchise owners requested and volunteered to pioneer a new service delivery system as part of their remodel. Both Brooks Barrett in Fairfield, Connecticut, and John Boujoukas in Natick, Massachusetts, had marketing backgrounds before becoming franchise owners: Brooks on Madison Avenue and John with Dunkin' Donuts. Their notion was to replace the twenty-seat question mark counter with a self-service counter and the porcelain cups used in-store with a 100 percent paper coffee service. The space now vacated by the twenty-seat counter could be used for tables and chairs or booths with padded seats. In-store coffee consumers would now line up in front of a counter and be served by a salesperson with coffeemakers in front of them.

Brooks and John's hope was to expedite service and eliminate the noise, mess, and bottleneck of the dishwashing machine required to clean the cups. This era was also characterized by a tight labor market; franchisees wished to get by with fewer staff, and a drive-through window was another must-have in these newly reconfigured shops.

The quick-service food industry was built on two factors: convenience and value. The trade-off in our new system was that while we might potentially gain in convenience by relinquishing porcelain cups, a less personal contact with the customer might diminish perceived value. Nevertheless, we decided to proceed with the experiment and the stores were remodeled. It didn't take long for the verdict to come in. Customers liked the added convenience and sales responded accordingly. We quickly adapted all new builds and remodels to this new configuration and service delivery system.

But change can be difficult for some to accept. It wasn't long after we began to convert to this new self-service system that I was interviewed on an afternoon talk show in Boston. Jerry Williams, known as the dean and early pioneer of the talk show format, was on WRKO in Boston for decades with a listenership of over a hundred thousand people per day. I was lucky enough to be his guest one afternoon to discuss Dunkin' Donuts and franchising opportunities. Turns out, I was bombarded and lambasted by scores of irate customers. They called in to express their outrage at the elimination of the counter and cups. "My life is not the same since you changed," one caller said. Another told me, "I'm never going into another one of your stores again." Few, if any as I recall, were interested in the life-changing opportunities franchising could offer. They were intent in telling the guy in the studio how he had impacted their lives by changing their routine. It was one tough afternoon, but I came away with a very clear view of the role we played in the everyday life of millions of people. You might think, "What the heck, it's just a cup of coffee," but these people cared deeply about the entire experience of buying their morning coffee. It is a lesson I never forgot.

Luckily, most customers got over the change and returned. Slowly but surely, these changes—the reconfiguration, drive-through windows, and remote seating—began to transform our business over the next decade from primarily a donut shop to a coffee shop, as sales inverted from 40 percent beverages and 60 percent bakery goods to 60–40, with beverages now the driver of the business.

3. Broadened Distribution

The second seismic shift in our business model came about in 1983. I traveled to Japan to mend fences with Seibu after our efforts in the courts had stalled, then on to the Philippines and Thailand to visit our nascent operations, thus far being reported as successful. I also had to convince the Philippine franchise holders not to sell donuts in unauthorized kiosks in movie theaters and gas stations around

Manila. It was argued at our operating committee meeting that "stretching the Dunkin' Donut brand to nonproducing sites threatened product freshness and thereby the integrity of the brand." Those were chilling words for a company that had staked its future on donuts made fresh every four hours, one striving to stay true to Fred the Baker's admonition: "You can bet supermarkets don't make their donuts fresh like we do."

I had invited Tom to join me on this trip and met him in Tokyo. The goal was to reset our relationship with Seibu, then travel on to Manila. The meeting with Seibu was civil but did little to motivate them to warm to the fight with Mister Donut.

At the same time, I was eager to get a firsthand view of the competition. In keeping with my practice of knowing my competitors, I maintained very friendly conversations over the years with the management of Duskin, the Mister Donut franchise holder, when we met at the annual International Franchise Association conventions in the US. I contacted Duskin and told them of my plans to visit Japan, requesting a meeting at their headquarters. Their response was warm; an invitation was extended. This meeting proved to be one of the more memorable occasions of my time at Dunkin.

Tom and I took the *shinkansen* bullet train from Tokyo to their headquarters in Osaka. As we approached their modern facilities, we were surprised and overwhelmed as hundreds of their staff stood on balconies or hung out of windows applauding our arrival. A huge banner that read, "Welcome Mr. Bob Rosenberg, CEO, and Mr. Tom Schwarz, COO, of Dunkin' Donuts" hung over the facade of their building. We felt like rock stars! This warm and open reception gave ample evidence that the basis of their business culture, "to be of service to others," wasn't just a slogan. At the same time, it became clearer why this company was such a fierce and able competitor. Remember, this was the very same company that obligated their prospective franchisees to knock on doors and offer to clean the resident's bathroom, the goal being to determine whether the prospect had a strong enough orientation to serve and therefore to be a fit for Duskin.

After our day in Osaka, Tom and I continued to Manila. Our Philippine franchise holders consisted of two families: the Prietos and the Spakowskis. Both families had a number of friends who also invested in the franchise. Leo Prieto was from an established Spanish family and had lived in the Philippines since the days of the Spanish conquest of this now nearly 100-million-people archipelago. The Spakowskis maintained a home in Hartford, Connecticut. Leo spoke for the licensees and was a very impressive man. Among his many achievements, he was the commissioner of basketball in the Philippines, a hugely successful sport there.

Leo was aware that my mission was to put an end to the nonapproved distribution system developed in Manila, but he wisely never broached the subject. As I was to discover during my visit, this system of delivering and selling donuts and coffee under the Dunkin' Donuts name in kiosks was created and driven by the wives of the board members. The board families were among the wealthiest and best connected in Manila. These spouses were using their connections to gain prime sites for their kiosks in high-traffic areas such as convenience stores and movie theaters, enlisting their household staff to deliver donuts by jitney and to staff the kiosks. Most of these small stands were open for limited hours, sourcing donuts from the few producing shops open in Manila. Most importantly, the wives were pocketing some rather substantial profits.

In addition to visiting shops, there were two special occasions planned during our time in the Philippines. One was for me to participate in a series of ceremonies launching a small warehouse and distribution center as well as a Dunkin' Donuts University classroom. Another was a formal dinner to acknowledge and celebrate team members' achievements. All the board members and, of course, their wives were invited.

The first evening, I was provided with my own embroidered Barong, the traditional Philippine men's shirt, and I dispensed coins to the attendees in what was a standard christening ritual. That evening, a number of wives came up to talk to me, relating in chapter and verse their successes with their kiosks. The second night, during a sit-down dinner, I was conveniently seated between two wives who also spent the evening educating me about the advantages of their distribution system. They pleaded with me not to put an end to their businesses. I didn't have the heart to turn them down and told them I'd take it under advisement. The fact was, their experience was compelling.

On the plane to Bangkok and all the way back to the United States, Tom and I talked nonstop about Manila and the kiosks. What if we were to run with branded, nonproducing outlets? What would that new world look like? At that time, our standard shop measured approximately two thousand square feet, half of which was kitchen. We were paying prime retail rent for that space. What would unit economics look like if we opened in just one-thousand-square-foot retail spaces and relied on existing kitchens for our bakery goods? The looming questions were: Wouldn't product quality suffer—breaking our freshness pledge—if we shipped baked products and donuts in vans to branded outlets? If so, what could we do to minimize freshness degrading in shipping? What happens to the customer who comes into the store and expects that hot honey-dipped donut? How would we make sure that person is satisfied under this new delivery model? We were making all our products by hand in a nineteenth-century craft way. If we moved to a more centralized production, was it possible to transition to more consistent semiautomated equipment, maintaining or possibly even improving product quality?

All of these questions were swirling in our heads as we returned to headquarters. As luck would have it, Brooks Barrett, our franchise owner from Fairfield, Connecticut, once again petitioned us to alter the existing system. This time, Brooks wanted to open kiosks under the Dunkin' name in four commuter rail stations. Our response was an emphatic *yes*. In no time and with a minimal investment, he opened the hundred-square-foot kiosks. In thirty-five hours of operation per week, each kiosk enjoyed excellent sales and profits. There was no adverse effect on his existing producing store.

The exceptional results in Manila and Connecticut were enough for us to rethink our concept and how we'd go to market. We decided to revolutionize our distribution system. Rather than sell a franchise owner a single producing store, our plan would be to sell a territory with a planned development schedule in order for the franchisee to retain exclusivity. And rather than building a distribution system where we relied solely on customers coming to our store, we planned to take our products to wherever people worked, shopped, traveled, or played. For us this new thinking was as revolutionary and transformational as I imagine it was for Coca-Cola when they decided to bottle their product for universal distribution rather than rely on customers being able to have a Coke only at a soda fountain.

Tom went to work with Jack Shafer, then head of development, to create new contracts and redefine trade areas in each market for exclusive territories. Jack and his team put on a full-court press, seeking out qualified franchisees for these new territories. He created a new department to pursue locations on toll roads, colleges, and airports. They formed relationships with Marriott Host and Automatic Retailers, who controlled a good deal of the catering market in these venues. They designed portable kiosks that smartly vended beverages and bakery products and centralized semiautomated kitchens to service each territory. They even devised commissaries that could be cooperatively owned by several nearby territorial holders, if that made sense, selecting delivery vans and devising packing techniques to minimize staling during transport.

Yes, we had to make some trade-offs, such as sacrificing the warm honey dip for the few customers who might have been lucky enough to get there when the product was hot out of the kitchen. But the gain in terms of providing customers more convenience in accessing our product was inestimable. Not to mention the benefit of less reliance on the scarce, skilled donut baker needed in each and every store. As we expanded, the lack of available bakers was becoming a growing problem and a limiting factor for our growth. This issue also impacted our ability to attract better businesspeople to our franchise.

The by-product of this transformation was a dramatic change in the economic return for our franchise owners. A stand-alone store might have a return on investment of 12–15 percent, but a network of a producing site combined with many nonproducing satellites might increase that return for the network by as much as 50 percent. Our new-store opening program quickly grew from one hundred a year to almost two hundred, all with a greater margin of safety than ever before.

With these new favorable unit economics, the strong franchisees began to buy up the weaker ones and add to their adjacent network and commissary. Up until that time, unit economics stalled the creation of large franchisee networks. Prior to this transformation, the largest network under one owner was eight stores. With every store having a kitchen and producing product, it was difficult for an owner to pay a manager a competitive wage and still have enough left over for a fair return on his capital. With this new distribution system, it was not unusual to see networks of twenty, thirty, and even a few on course to one hundred units.

I remember how proud I was at a franchisee convention to have Carlos Andrade, the franchise owner of more than a hundred Dunkin' Donuts stores, stand as I told the audience, "Carlos now owns more stores than the total size of the chain when I assumed the presidency of Dunkin' Donuts in 1963." The Dunkin' Donuts franchise was becoming a vehicle for not only creating a better standard of living for its franchisees and their families, but now also provided an opportunity to become a multimillionaire as well.

4. The Territorial License for Chili's

The fourth initiative was furthest afield from our core business. Our models were projecting dwindling earnings growth. Our sales and observations indicated that many of our customers preferred casual dining restaurants to fast food. A number of other fast-food companies saw the same trends. In response, they began to add casual dining concepts to their repertoire over the ensuing years. McDonald's bought the sixteen-unit Chipotle Mexican Grills, along with the faltering Boston Market. Mickey D's also bought Aroma Café, a twenty-three-unit food and coffee chain from the United Kingdom. Pillsbury, parent company of Burger King, purchased Steak and Ale and launched Bennigan's. That trend continued for many years after. Wendy's bought Baja Fresh for $275 million in 2002, and Jack in the Box acquired Qdoba for $45 million in 2003.

Given our past failed experience in trying to launch a fish and chips chain on our own in the late 1960s, starting a chain from scratch held no appeal for me. I reasoned it was too risky and time consuming to try and create a concept with a unique offering—odds for start-ups could be as high as 100 to 1.

Since my natural inclination was to edge out rather than bet the ranch when encountering a big change, I instead championed the purchase of exclusive rights for a large chunk of the US from what I considered to be the best casual dining chain in the industry: Chili's. I reasoned that by buying into a proven franchise, we could hit the ground running. And if for any reason we wanted to exit, we had a ready buyer in the parent company.

Chili's was primarily a company-owned operation and had yet to expand into the Northeast or Canada. But they sold franchise rights in other areas like Florida where they did not expect to expand for many years. In our many stays in Florida, my family and I were frequent customers, so I witnessed firsthand their unique menu and great service delivery system. I was also well aware of the reputation and success of the chain's founder, Norman Brinker.

Brinker was a legend in the restaurant industry. A true innovator and mentor of talent, he was successful at everything he touched. Of all things, he started out as a member of the US equestrian team and competed in the 1952 Olympics in Helsinki. While attending college, he met and married Maureen Connolly. Maureen, known as "Little Mo," was one of the greatest female tennis players of all time: the winner of nine Grand Slam singles titles in the 1950s. After college, Norman helped launch Jack in the Box in San Diego, followed by the first casual dining chain known as Steak and Ale, where he offered the first salad bar. He sold Steak and Ale to Pillsbury, becoming president of their restaurant division. There he was responsible for not only Burger King but the creation of the Bennigan's concept as well. He left Pillsbury to buy a six-store chain in Dallas called Chili's, broadening the menu and staffing the organization with talent. His success was not limited to commercial ventures. Maureen Connolly died at age thirty-four of cancer. In 1982, Norman and his new wife, Nancy, formed the Susan G. Komen foundation in honor of Nancy's sister Susan, who had also died of breast cancer. Their fundraising effort has been one of the most successful in the battle against cancer, raising $2 billion to date.

We formed a subsidiary called Dunkin' Ventures, which was designed to find and operate new opportunities in these fast emerging and growing segments of the away-from-home food industry. After twenty-five years of focusing solely on coffee and donut shops, we were starting to expand into a portfolio of food service businesses. It was no secret among senior management that I wanted to start with Chili's. I wanted to be associated with Norman Brinker and learn the secrets of casual dining from the organization I considered the best in the field. We negotiated an agreement to be the exclusive licensee for Chili's in the New England states, eastern Canada, and upstate New York, a territory that included nearly forty million people. If we were successful making this transition, we had sufficient geography to open at least a hundred restaurants, possibly more. With that number of stores, profits could amount to $20 million per year, matching our earnings for our existing business in 1985, the year we struck the agreement.

By 1988, we had opened ten Chili's restaurants, which enjoyed outstanding consumer acceptance. Sales were averaging well above $2 million per restaurant—north of the average for the system as a whole and demonstrating the southwestern menu was embraced by New Englanders. As a rule, an established franchise business has the advantage of being highly cash generative. As a result, from our core business we had the ability to issue dividends and buy back our stock as well as fund our capital needs to grow our restaurants. We were on target. In 1987, we were able to post an increase in earnings per share of 14 percent despite having to cover a $2.9 million loss as a result of our start-up of Chili's, funding a new organization, and the infrastructure necessary to grow that business. That loss was reduced to $1.9 million in the subsequent year, and we were on track to turn profitable by 1990.

As the 1980s came to an end, we were pleased we had put into motion initiatives that would drive growth and achieve our objectives for the coming decade.

ORGANIZATION

No story of Dunkin' Donuts would be complete without telling the story of its franchise owners. Although they may not be on the payroll of the parent company, their contributions cannot be overestimated.

Especially in the early years, it was their courage and willingness to bet their capital on a new business idea combined with hard work that lit a fire under our company. Like most start-ups, we relied on family and friends to invest, especially in the early days. After my father purchased my uncle's 50 percent of the business in 1955, we had no cash with which to expand our five-store donut chain. We were heavily in debt. First to step up was the company's labor lawyer, Maury Epstein, who had helped my dad negotiate union contracts with the route drivers of his Industrial Luncheon Service. Maury knew of the success of the early donut shops and had confidence in my dad, investing $100,000 to open the first three franchised shops. He would own 50 percent and my father would own the other half, paying Maury back out of the profits. He was quickly followed by Barney Ackman, a friend of my father's from his days at the shipyard during the war. He and his partner opened a very successful store in Dedham, Massachusetts. Learning of his success, fellow cab drivers followed suit after Barney sold his medallion.

The American Dream

The rapid growth of the chain through franchising in the 1970s and '80s was powered by first-generation immigrants primarily from South Asia, the Azores, and Greece. These were people leaving their homeland for a better opportunity in America. Today as many as 60 percent of the nearly 9,500 US stores are owned by descendants of those early and courageous pioneers.

After volcanic eruptions on the small island of San Miguel in the Portuguese archipelago forced him to leave for a better opportunity, Manny Andrade immigrated to New England, finding work as a donut maker in the New Bedford Dunkin' Donuts shop. Yes, the very same location that was about to close its doors as a food donut shop my first week as CEO of the company.

Manny worked hard and saved his money. In 1975, he purchased his own franchise in Rhode Island, proving right away he was very good at running his business. As he began to see how success was possible and within reach, he began to spread the news to family members. Tony Andrade, Manny's brother, was only seventeen when he came to this country. Other relatives followed, including his brother-in-law, each of them joining the burgeoning Andrade donut chain until they could save enough money to buy a store of their own. When the Andrades ran out of relatives in San Miguel, they encouraged others from the town to join them.

These former citizens of the Azores demonstrated a penchant for hard work and a real skill at running a retail business. Many settled in Rhode Island and proved to be able not only to run the system as designed by the company but to improve on it as well. These were the franchise owners who first experimented with additional advertising. This led to the contract revision that doubled the contractual ad spend, putting the brand squarely on the map.

Tony Andrade began to open stores and sell them to highly qualified employees using ten-year mortgages. He also owned most of the real estate where his thirty-six-store chain was sited. Tony had an eye for talent and integrity; when he lent a qualified employee the money to buy a franchise, these loans were repaid in full and on time. These days, Tony has sold a number of his stores and retired to Florida with a net worth—recently reported to the *Boston Globe*—of more than $50 million.

Fernando Cafua, a baker for Tony, hailed from the same village of Vila Franca on San Miguel. Fernando and his wife, Gilda, eventually purchased their own Dunkin' Donuts shop from Tony in Derry, New Hampshire. Today, their son Mark and his brothers have expanded their network to include more than three hundred Dunkin' restaurants in several states, generating a substantial amount in annual sales. This is how mighty oaks grow from little acorns!

The same story repeated itself in the Midwest as we began to expand there: this time the heroes were from India, Pakistan, and Bangladesh. Here, too, first-generation immigrants came to America in search of new opportunity, finding it in the operation of a retail donut and coffee shop.

The transition for some foreign-born entrepreneurs wasn't as seamless in Chicago as it was in New England. There were times when Old-World standards were perpetuated and the businesses suffered as a result. But as the next generation—now native-born and often business-school trained—assumed responsibility for the family stores, standards and results soared.

Many of these pioneering franchise owners were partnerships. The long hours of operation, the demands of creating handcrafted products, and the cash nature of the business required lots of day-to-day management. Often, these successful partnerships comprised a husband and wife team: a real mom-and-pop business. For example, John and Rose Padussis built a very high-volume shop in Glen Burnie, Maryland. Their success made for a great human-interest story, picked up and carried by *Reader's Digest*. George and Peggy Clapp, originally from Cambridge, Massachusetts, had to move to a dry climate for health reasons. Peggy's dad, Bob Stewart, had suffered smoke damage to his lungs from his years with the Cambridge Fire Department. So they pulled up stakes and moved as a family to Tucson, Arizona, where they opened several successful stores over the years.

Early franchise owners also came out of our parent company's middle manager ranks. Owners like John Boujoukas, the pioneer in our move to paper cups and self-service, was once an executive with the company, as was Randy Plante, Steve Gabellieri, Gorge Zografos, and Ed Bailey. All became very successful franchise owners.

Today, 90 percent of all new Dunkin' Donuts shops that open in the United States are owned by existing franchisees. This fact stands as indisputable evidence of the courage, skills, ingenuity, and hard work of the early franchisees who joined and persevered before broadened distribution, off-site commissaries, and improved store configuration transformed the concept.

This story of success was recounted with great accuracy and heart by the cable business channel CNBC in their December 3, 2010, hour-long special entitled "Behind the Counter." CNBC chronicled the highs and lows of the then $600-billion-a-year franchise business. The program highlighted the progress of two families in the Chicago market that started modestly with one store but—in just one generation—mushroomed into small donut empires. In 2015, 80 percent of greater Chicagoland's more than three hundred Dunkin' Donuts shops were owned by families originally hailing from Southeast Asia: the Bangladesh Padjwani family being one of them. From the one store Sam Padjwani and his wife began in 1988, they now have thirty-three restaurants along with their two sons, Amin and Ali.

The Shah family from India is also a remarkable success story. Their Dunkin' chain numbers six stores, forming part of a bakery cooperative owned by thirty-nine separate Chicago Dunkin' franchisees that support the daily bakery needs of more than three hundred Dunkin' stores within a fifty-mile radius of their hundred thousand-square-foot facility, employing more than 280 people.

The CNBC piece closes by stating that "Dunkin' Donuts' current ad campaign reminds its consumers that 'America runs on Dunkin'.' But it's important to remember that Dunkin'—the company—runs on the American Dream."

COMMUNICATION AND CRISIS MANAGEMENT

The year 1989 was to prove one of the most dangerous in the company's history. Risks to the business and its franchise owners rivaled the near-death experience posed by the class action suit fifteen years earlier. The events of that year were to challenge me personally by thrusting me into a world of high finance and public attention I had never before experienced.

The signs began in early March. Our stock price for no apparent reason had begun to climb from the mid-$20 per share to the low $30s. At first, I thought it might have been due to speculation that we were being bought by Pepsi Cola. Pepsi had entered the burgeoning away-from-home food business to supplement their package goods grocery store business. They had purchased Pizza Hut, Taco Bell, and Kentucky Fried Chicken. Pepsi had also been a major beverage supplier to our system. I was their guest at Super Bowl XXIII held in late January in Miami. My wishful thinking was, "Analysts may have seen me in the Pepsi box and assumed Dunkin' was a good fit with those other brands and we were in discussions to be bought by Pepsi."

There was another possible reason that might explain this higher stock price—one more difficult to face. The last five years had been marked by a rash of hostile takeover and greenmail attempts across the American business scene. Since 1988, in Massachusetts alone, the Stop and Shop Companies were pursued by the Dart Group, forcing a leverage buyout. Computervision lost its independence in a bid from Prime Computer. Gillette won a proxy fight to remain independent against predator Ron Perelman and Coniston Partners, and Polaroid maintained its independence from Shamrock Holdings, an acquisition entity formed by the Disney family. Polaroid had successfully created an employee stock ownership program, an ESOP, to thwart the unwanted advances of Shamrock.

This boom in hostile takeovers was spurred, at least in part, by a significant change in the profile of those who owned America's corporations since the days we went public in 1968. Historically, capitalism was founded and built on what I would call patient capital: companies were founded and supported by individual investors who believed in the long-term prospect of an enterprise.

Before 1945, only 5 percent of equities was managed by institutional investors. That percentage grew to 34 percent by 1980 and mushroomed to more than 70 percent by 2010. As Knowledge@

Wharton reported, "This trend is in part due to the increased importance of retirement plans in recent decades and the resulting delegation of portfolio management to institutions."[1]

Institutional investment managers are compensated and promoted based on the returns they earn on their portfolio. With that in mind, you can imagine how impossible it is for the institutional investor to turn away from the often 40 percent overnight appreciation that occurs when a company is put in play. That 40 percent generally reflects the value added when control of a company is in balance. If a company is under attack, institutional investors rarely wait until a transaction occurs. Not wanting to risk the deal not getting done, they sell their shares to "arbs" (arbitrageurs). Arbs have no interest in the long-term prospects of the business. They are betting the last pennies of a deal on a transaction occurring.

The courts also contributed to the increase in hostile takeovers. Despite a company having many constituents, including employees, customers, communities, and in our case, franchise owners, the courts historically ruled on the supremacy of the stockholder over all other constituents. Companies were seen as maximizing shareholder return as their only mission—which put managers in a veritable straightjacket. If a time came where management felt the need to sacrifice short-term earnings for longer-term gains, predators could pounce and—in tight legal maneuvers attendant to these fights—the courts supported the attacker who promised short-term stock gains.

A great deal of this takeover activity was spawned by Drexel Burnham Lambert investment bank's financial whiz Michael Milken. He was known for his use of previously little used high-risk junk bond financings for hostile takeovers. Milken was able to produce a "highly confident letter" to promise that these highly leveraged deals could actually be financed. Corporate raiders such as T. Boone Pickens and Carl Ichan used these in their bids for major oil companies, as did Ted Turner in his buyout bid for MGM. Kohlberg Kravis's successful bid for RJR (Reynold's Tobacco) is another illustration of the rampant predatory behavior that marked these years. In view of this, we had asked our bankers, Goldman Sachs, to prepare us in the event we were struck. We took the standard steps to position ourselves to slow down unwanted bids and ensure stockholders the best price if, in fact, we were the target of an unwanted bid.

Reality struck hard in early March when a friend and former business school classmate, Peter Solomon, paid me a visit. We'd kept up our friendship after school, and I had followed his career. Peter went to work for Lehman Brothers after graduation and rose to be vice chair of that firm and head of its investment banking arm. In 1989, he decided to start his own firm and provide old-time advisory services to companies. Peter sat at the edge of my desk and told me what I had secretly feared: "Rosey, someone is buying up your stock and you are going to be the target of a hostile attack"—a potentially life-altering change for our company and for me, at least for the foreseeable future.

As the blood drained back into my body, Peter went on to say: "I'm starting a bank to provide advisory services to senior managers, like the good old days at Goldman when managing partners such as Gus Levy and Sidney Weinberg sat alongside corporate CEOs and provided them with financial and strategic advice. Today, investment banks are like silos moving you from one specialized department to the next. There is no continuity, and you don't always get the bank's best thinking. Oftentimes, lower-ranking associates are not necessarily interested in what is best for the long-term interests of the company, only in the big money that happens when a transaction occurs. I think I can help you, and you could be my first client."

I didn't mind that Peter was making a sales call. In fact, I was comforted by the notion of having him by my side. He was a friend of twenty-five years; I respected and trusted him. He was bringing me information that my bankers on Wall Street had not.

I shared Peter's proposal with senior managers, my board, and Goldman Sachs, finally receiving board permission to retain Peter J. Solomon Company as an advisor alongside Goldman. The senior managers as well as our account manager from Goldman ramped up a plan to establish an ESOP: an employee stock ownership plan. We had been considering this alternative for a while, confident that this was a way to place more company shares in the hands of our employees who understood that we were more interested in the long-term well-being of the company than some corporate raider. An ESOP was also a good way to provide additional motivation to our team toward the achievement of our long-term financial goals.

An employee stock ownership program is a method for a company to sell shares to its employees' retirement accounts. The government, to encourage employee ownership, allows tax-deductible payments by the corporation, up to 25 percent of its payroll, to the ESOP to service the payment for those shares. An ESOP had earlier been employed by Polaroid in its tussle with Disney.

I had resisted pulling the trigger on an ESOP earlier because it would require us to lay off around eighty of our six hundred staff to service the loan. The thought of a layoff was anathema to me: I had always viewed our staff as family. But faced with the possibility of a raider buying and destroying the company and the life and dreams of hundreds of our franchise owners and their families, I acceded to the plan. We would issue 1.1 million shares at the current market price of $35 per share to an employee stock plan owned by our employees. The cost to pay for this transaction in interest and principal would cost the company $4.5 million per year for fifteen years until the debt was retired. The shares amounted to approximately 16 percent ownership in the company. My family and my father had sold most, if not all, of their stock in the twenty years we were publicly owned. This 16 percent plus the approximately 9 percent owned or under option by me, management, and the board, we reasoned, should be a deterrent to a hostile raider.

Our board's first order of business on Tuesday morning, April 11, 1989, was to vote on the establishment of the ESOP. As we sat in the boardroom, we were interrupted by the news from Goldman that Knightsbridge Capital, a Canadian investment banking firm and a division of Unicorp, had just filed a 13D.[2] It had already promised to be a fateful day, but this put it over the top. We had just divvied up among our five senior managers and me the names of each person slated to be laid off. After the vote, we were to talk to each person face-to-face explaining that their layoff was not due to something they had done but because certain positions were being eliminated. We were not eliminating any field jobs associated with new-store development or operations; rather, we were focusing on what we felt were less essential staff jobs. It was our intent to maintain each person's dignity and explain as best we could our Sophie's choice. We were also providing outplacement help to get them relocated in new jobs with other companies. Finally, we planned for me to meet with small groups at the home office to explain our plan and for some senior managers to fly to our zone offices to explain, in person, the new direction we had taken.

But the latest news came as a cold slap across the face. We sat in the boardroom stunned. I remember someone musing, "What crazy timing. Had we met a day or two earlier we might have staved off the filing." Someone else asked, "Who is Knightsbridge Capital?" It wasn't long before Goldman started to fill us in.

Knightsbridge was a newly formed division of Unicorp, the fifteenth largest company in Canada. Unicorp itself was also new, created to hold the assets of Union Gas of Canada, its major asset. The recent Union Gas takeover was highly controversial; in fact, it was being investigated by the Toronto Stock Exchange and the Canadian Securities Board in Ontario. Unicorp had also just purchased Lincoln Savings in New York City, while another division held some real estate in the US. Unicorp was headed by George Mann, a Toronto real estate developer and a known greenmailer, a term used to describe someone who buys shares in a company with the intent of bidding the price up only to sell his shares back to the company at a profit in exchange for going away. Mann had, years previous, made a play for Purolator courier but went away after the company bought his shares for a sizable profit.

I mused aloud, "Why would a gas utility company and savings bank have an interest in an American donut franchisor? How are they going to add value?" But the die was cast. All we could do was to put in place the ESOP and brace for Knightsbridge's next move.

The day was heartbreaking in so many ways. Most painful were the talks with our comrades with whom we were soon to part. To their credit, they were all understanding and wished us luck. The small group meetings in the home offices were painful as well; people were concerned about their jobs. I had to be reassuring and quell their fears.

That night, as might be expected, was a sleepless one. Next morning at seven sharp, I had a breakfast meeting with Chad Gifford, CEO of Bank of Boston, our longtime commercial bankers. Chad couldn't have been more supportive, and in just an hour I walked from the bank with a commitment for $38 million to fund the ESOP. When I returned to the office, word had arrived that Knightsbridge would not be deterred by our ESOP and was intent on gaining control of our company. Earl Rotman, head of Knightsbridge Capital, had called and left word he wanted to talk.

Some fateful decisions were made during a meeting of our operating committee held that afternoon. We agreed that I, along with Tom Schwarz and Larry Hantman, our general counsel, would spend all of our time addressing the hostile attack, while the remainder of the senior managers would operate the business day to day.

Phone calls were now pouring in from the press. Questions had to be answered. PBS's *Nightly Business Report* requested an interview that very afternoon to be aired on the evening news. These were the days before cable business news; I reasoned that most financial analysts and executives would watch the *Nightly Business Report* and that this was the best way to reach our shareholders and encourage them to stick with us. It was the only daily TV show that featured financial news at the time.

The daily newspapers wanted interviews as well. The *Boston Globe* and the *Globe and Mail* from Toronto wanted to talk as did the *Boston Record-American*. We had not yet retained a law firm specializing in takeovers, so I turned to my fellow board member Archie Southgate for advice on how to respond to all these inquiries.

As always, his advice was sound: "You should tell the public you see no reason to talk to Knightsbridge. If you did, it would indicate you are interested in making a deal. Look, they bought some stock and came after us. We didn't put the company up for sale. The board and management believe our past record of shareholder returns and future prospects make the company a lot more valuable than the current market price. At least for now we can use the 'just say no' defense. But you have to be careful your remarks are not interpreted to show that resistance to a deal is to merely entrench management."

And with that I began months of dealing with the media.

As the days went by, rumors swirled. Earl Rotman of Knightsbridge reported to the press their plan to sell off the home office property in Randolph, Massachusetts, as well as our fifteen Chili's restaurants. It seemed Unicorp owned a partially occupied building on Tremont Street in Boston, and their plan was to relocate us from our headquarters to their building. Others speculated that Unicorp couldn't raise the more than $300 million most felt the business was worth. It was posited that Mann planned to sell off the real estate we still had on the books and on which hundreds of stores were operating. I saw little liquidation value of that real estate, however, since all of it was occupied by franchisees under long-term leases.

The next week, Peter Solomon came to pay me another visit. He told me the following: "It doesn't appear these guys are in it for greenmail. It seems that, for whatever reason, they really want to buy the company. They've already made a $15 million investment in the shares but haven't made an offer to buy all the shares yet. I'm not sure if it's because they haven't nailed down the financing, but in any event, I have a plan that may thwart that."

My ears perked up.

He continued: "We can offer convertible preferred shares to a long-term investor who has confidence in your long-term prospects. We can contact financial entities to see if they are interested in making a $35 million investment in convertible preferred stock, which pays a dividend but can be convertible for seven years if the stock goes over $40. That would convert to seven hundred thousand voting shares, and we can stipulate a commitment they will vote with you. Proceeds from the sale of the preferred shares can be used to buy back another 10 percent of the shares."

I had to ask, "Is that legal?" He assured me it was.

"Okay," I said. "If I understand this right, this means that if it ever came to a final vote, we can count on up to 40 percent of the shares to support our long-term plans. And we may still be able to gain additional support from individual shareholders."

Peter had explained to me that in the event of an all-cash offer deemed "adequate," all institutional shareholders would sell their shares. In fact, when such an offer is made, most institutionally held shares would migrate to arbitrageurs.

I brought Peter's plan to Goldman and my board. All agreed it made sense, and Goldman began to develop an offering circular. We were ready to circulate the offering by the beginning of May. Fred Krimendahl, the Goldman partner, suggested we approach Warren Buffett with the deal; we all agreed he'd be perfect. He already owned Dairy Queen and liked to be involved with businesses like retail franchises that have a perceived moat around them because of their brand strength.

Buffett had been visiting Martha Stewart that weekend at her summer home. The offering circular was delivered but he declined quickly, saying, "I don't buy in the middle of a takeover fight and, further, the deal isn't sizable enough for me." We were very disappointed, but luckily that didn't last long. Within a week, General Electric Credit liked the offering and was prepared to buy the $35 million convertible preferred. We sealed the deal before the end of May, announced it to the press, and began to buy back shares. My hope now was that Mann would capitulate and sell his shares into the $35 million buyback we had launched. I was buoyed, at least temporarily, when I read that Mann, when asked what he would do in light of this move, responded, "I can't decide whether I'm a buyer or a seller."

We didn't have to wait very long for his decision. Mann made a formal offer to the board to purchase the company for $42 per share to be paid mostly in cash but in some notes as well. They had to provide a "highly confident" letter from a reliable financing institution that financing for this offer was secured. The takeover was now becoming much more real. That move forced us to turn to our bankers for an "adequacy" assessment. Goldman had to evaluate if the offer was adequate or fair; if not, we could reject it as "inadequate." The evaluation took a week or so. Goldman deemed the offer, because of its contingencies in payment, as inadequate. The board voted unanimously to reject the offer.

Throughout this whole process, the Dunkin' Donuts franchisees were becoming increasingly concerned about their future and how the hostile takeover would affect them. Unlike the disenchanted Burger King franchise owners who only a year before had supported Grand Metropolitan's takeover of their brand from Pillsbury, the Dunkin' owners were happy with their franchisor and sought no such change.

In early May, a group of franchise leaders came to headquarters. I suggested they retain an attorney and take whatever steps they felt were legal and necessary to protect themselves. They hired a fine Boston attorney, Ken Novack, who was a partner in the prestigious Mintz Levin firm. Ken later became the vice chairman of AOL, but at the time, he helped the franchisees form the Dunkin' Donuts Independent Franchise Association. They raised funds as well as wrote letters to Knightsbridge strongly voicing their opposition to the takeover. On May 24, 1989, they took out a full-page ad in the *Wall Street Journal* telling the world they were seventeen hundred strong and opposed to the takeover, and they listed all the reasons they had faith in current management and the direction of the company.

On June 15, Knightsbridge announced that they had joined forces with Cara Operations, a publicly owned food service company in Canada, and they were making a tender offer of $43 per share in cash and notes effective once they accumulated 75 percent of the shares outstanding. They now apparently had the financing for at least a portion of the purchase price and had a credible food service operator as a partner.

Cara was founded by the Phalen family in Canada in the 1860s to sell newspapers and sundries at Canadian Railways stations, ergo the name Cara, a contraction of Canadian Railway. Cara had grown more recently by opening some retail fast-food and casual dining chains in Canada. It was hard to tell if this was their plan all along, but matters seemed to be rapidly coming to a head and the outcome was very much in doubt.

Because the tender offer was not all cash but a combination of cash and notes, Knightsbridge received only another 15 percent of the shares tendered. By now they owned 12 percent of the shares. Their shares combined with the 15 percent tendered were still far short of control. They extended their offer for another two weeks. Same result: stockholders were not interested, concluding that their prospects looked brighter with the existing company than throwing in their lot with Knightsbridge and Cara—at least as it compared with the current offer.

Finally, in early September, Knightsbridge and Cara converted their offer to $43 all cash. We could no longer just say no, or consider their offer "inadequate." After a valiant five-month battle we were being forced to put the company up for sale—a crushing blow to all of us. The objective now quickly shifted to finding the best possible buyer to preserve all we had built. We wanted to find an owner who shared our values and vision for the future, and we were quite sure George Mann did not fit that bill.

Acquisitions generally fall into one of two categories: strategic buyers or financial buyers. A strategic buyer is an existing operating entity that buys a business usually to bolt onto its existing business, while a financial buyer is not generally looking to add to an existing business but uses its financial knowledge to assess an enterprise's worth and add value either by good management or financial engineering or a combination. While we were jousting with Knightsbridge and Mann, we decided to seek alternatives from both types of buyers.

Tom, Larry, and I began to seek and interview a number of private equity firms and cultivate the few strategic buyers who showed an interest. The first potential strategic buyer to show up was none other than our old friends and competitors from Japan, Duskin. They had made a major commitment to the food business and were now the owners of the rights to develop the Mister Donut brand throughout Asia.

I received a call from a well-known and much-admired McKinsey partner, Kenichi (Ken) Ohmae, who at the time headed up

McKinsey's consulting practice in Japan. Ken reminded me that he was my translator in the early 1970s while he was a student in Boston studying at MIT and I was negotiating our franchise for Japan with Seibu. Ken told me he now represented Duskin and related the company's plan was to arrange a loan from a major Japanese bank for the purchase price. Although Ken felt the loan would be no issue, Duskin's only condition was that I and our management team had to stay on to run the company for ten years until they got comfortable with business in the United States. I encouraged Ken to continue conversations. We were interested but until we got to the details could not promise all management would stay.

Goldman had sent letters to approximately fifty potential strategic buyers we thought might be a fit. At the time, America was living through a recession caused by the collapsing junk bond market and failure of the savings and loan industry. Stocks for US companies had yet to recover from the 23 percent drop they experienced on October 19, 1987, known as Black Monday. Most companies in the US were not in a buying mood. Other than Duskin, we had no interest from other strategic buyers.

During September and the first half of October, Tom, Larry, and I met with a number of private equity companies. Some showed up as a result of Goldman's offering circular. Others we solicited because of previous friendships. Len Harlan, partner in the private equity firm Castle Harlan, had been my fraternity brother at Cornell and had preceded me at Harvard Business School. Thomas H. Lee had been an associate on our account when he worked for Bank of Boston years earlier, before establishing the very successful private equity company bearing his name. We also met with Bruce Wasserstein of Wasserstein Perella. Both men had storied careers at First Boston before opening their own boutique private equity firm in 1988. We also reached out to San Francisco's Hellman Friedman firm, founded by Warren Hellman, who was previously with Lehman Brothers, and Tully Friedman, who had previously been with Solomon Brothers.

In the late 1980s, private equity was relatively unknown. There were not many firms active in this type of financing. The few stories

I had heard were about astounding rates of return. As I saw it, the early model for private equity investors was to put very little of their own money up, borrow most of the purchase price through high-yield junk bonds and mezzanine financing, mostly arranged through Milken, and seek returns as high as 35 to 50 percent. I reasoned that since they had few competitors, they could command these high returns.

In our case, I found myself parrying private equity investors' pressure to cut millions of dollars of costs out of the business in order to service their high and costly debt and achieve their targeted returns. (By way of contrast, the environment now is very different. Competition is quite fierce. There may be as many as two thousand private equity firms competing for deals. A private equity firm today may put up as much as 50 percent of the purchase price and finance the remaining 50 percent from banks or securitized bonds. Targeted returns are closer to 20 percent than 35 percent.) But at the time, we had just had a 16 percent reduction in staff. My team and I didn't have the heart for another round of significant layoffs. And more importantly, we felt we had cut staff to the bone; further reductions would only jeopardize the health of the business. For their part, many of the private equity firms were scared off by the run-up in the stock price due to the hostile attack. They didn't see a real bargain here and were cool to the deal as well. The Lee and Hellman firms passed on the deal as best as I can recall.

Duskin seemed to be having more of a problem arranging the $310 million–plus purchase price than they originally anticipated. It was becoming more difficult to reach Ken Ohmae on the phone until ultimately there was no communication at all. I concluded Duskin couldn't make the deal.

I had passed on a proxy fight with Knightsbridge for control of the company. My proxy solicitor tallied up the vote and informed me we would lose 51 percent to 49 percent. They told me we could count on 100 percent of the vote from our management team, the ESOP, and GE credit, 60 percent of the vote of individuals who owned stock in their own name, and 30 percent of those who owned in street name. But all the remaining institutional stockholders and

arbs would vote to take a $43 cash offer. As it turned out, my ac-
quaintance and early supporter Peter Lynch, who at one time owned
more than 15 percent of the company in his Fidelity Magellan Fund
and touted us as one of his great "ten baggers," had sold when the
price migrated to $40 a share.

My father had retired from the board four years earlier in 1985.
He left over a difference regarding the acquisition of the Chili's license. Shortly thereafter, he sold his remaining holdings of Dunkin'
Donuts stock. At the time, his ownership amounted to between 4
and 5 percent of the shares outstanding. Ironically, our proxy solicitor felt we could have won a proxy fight with George Mann and
avoided having to put the company up for sale had we been able to
count on another 2 percent of the stock voting with us.

If we took a risk and went for a vote, we could be caught in a two-
tiered offer. That meant if Knightsbridge did, in fact, buy 51 percent
of the stock at $43 per share, they would have control of the com-
pany and be able to make an offer for the remaining 49 percent at
a significantly lower price. It was too great a risk. I wasn't comfortable playing that kind of Russian roulette with the fortunes of my
employees and supporters.

Knightsbridge was pressing for an auction date and we had yet to
light on a satisfactory alternative. I set up another meeting with Peter Solomon at the 21 Club in New York City.

As we settled in for lunch, I said, "Peter, I am running out of alternatives. Do you have another suggestion?"

Much to my relief, he responded: "As a matter of fact, I do. You
might have been reading about how *Time* magazine is merging with
Warner Brothers to rid themselves of the hostile bid from Paramount Studios. They so complicated the acquisition they scared
Paramount off. Can you think of a merger or acquisition that makes
sense that might raise the price to Knightsbridge beyond what they
are prepared to pay or have financing available for?"

I said, "The only company that makes sense for us to buy is Mister
Donut, which International Multifoods owns." The era of large Min-
neapolis milling companies owning food service businesses in vogue

decades ago had long past. "They can't be too happy with the donut business; their prospects just aren't that bright."

"Why don't you call them?"

I assured him that I would call the Multifoods CEO the moment I returned to Boston. The response was quick and enthusiastic: they were very interested in selling the remaining 550 Mister Donut shops in the US.

The prospect of buying Mister Donut was exhilarating on so many levels. We'd finally end the donut wars begun thirty-five years earlier by my uncle Harry and my dad. We'd be buying our only major competitor in the US. We also might be on to a great investment. My belief was that our brand was so much stronger than theirs in most US markets that our purchase could add real value by re-branding the Mister Donut stores to Dunkin'. Finally, this might be a chance to rid ourselves of Knightsbridge. I was sure they hadn't bargained on paying for what promised to be twenty-three hundred stores rather than the seventeen hundred when the process started.

Tom put together a task force to look at the returns on investment at varying levels of purchase price. It seems we had converted a few Mister Donut shops in the last few years with significant improvement in store volume after the conversion. I felt confident I could make a presentation to my board that would demonstrate at least a 25 percent return on the acquisition, even if we had to pay north of $30 million for the chain. I was sure from preliminary conversations with Multifoods that the price would satisfy them. All that excitement came to a screeching halt when I proposed the deal to my board.

To finance the $30 million–plus purchase price, we would have to either issue stock or borrow from a bank, possibly tipping voting control in our favor. My board rejected the proposal despite its promise of a very high return. They feared it might embroil the company and themselves personally in litigation from both Knights-bridge and arbitrageurs for killing the Knightsbridge acquisition. It was a risk I could not convince them to take. I was crestfallen.

To top it all off, we were still without a satisfactory alternative and time was getting short. The court responded to Knightsbridge's request and established Friday November 10, 1989, as the date for an auction of the company.

My frustration over the fact that we hadn't been able to spark more interest in the company only grew. One company in particular puzzled me: Allied-Lyons, a large UK conglomerate that had bought one of our suppliers, DCA, a number of years earlier. They had also purchased Baskin-Robbins from United Fruit in the 1970s. Len Geller had informed me from time to time of the interest DCA's CEO, Dave Lipka, had in buying us. I had rejected his advances but now couldn't understand why they hadn't at least investigated. Len, Larry Hantman, and I flew to New York City to meet with Lipka.

When I asked Dave why they hadn't shown interest in view of his past offers, he replied, "I never discussed it with senior management in London. I was on a fishing expedition of my own to see if you had any interest. I thought if we did buy you, I could get all the donut mix business. I only have a part of the business now."

I informed him that our purchasing was conducted by franchisees and by bid, not by us directing to one supplier over another. I could not promise him the business, but by virtue of a closer relationship he could learn how to bid more effectively than he had in the past. Larry, Len, and I continued to show him how our business might fit into Allied's food business and how our know-how could benefit Baskin-Robbins. After a two-hour conversation, we got Lipka's commitment to present the opportunity to his boss, Tony Hales, in London. We flew back to Boston that night unsure of what Lipka would do. It was now late October and time was running out.

Much to my delight, within a few days I received a call from Lipka. Hales and the company's vice chairman, Richard Martin, wanted to fly over from England and meet within the week. Was I interested? You bet I was.

A few days later, Tony Hales and Richard Martin showed up at our headquarters and met with Tom, Larry, and Len Geller, followed by a four-hour, one-on-one meeting between Tony and me. We discussed all elements of the business and our plans for the future. He was ten years my junior. Before his current assignment as CEO of one of Allied's three main divisions, Hales had been a very successful managing director of one of their largest pub divisions. We were both retailers. We had a lot in common. I found him an incredibly likeable guy.

Hales liked our story and was excited about the prospects of buying Mister Donut, and I was intrigued by Allied's history of acting as a white knight and stepping in to save other great brands from the clutches of hostile predators. Only two years previous, they had stepped in at the last minute to buy the renowned Canadian spirits company Hiram Walker, headquartered in Windsor, Canada, and owner of such brands as Canadian Club, Courvoisier, and Kahlua, for $1.9 billion. It had been owned by the Hatch family since 1926 but was under attack from the Reichmann's, another powerful Canadian family, owners of Olympia and York Realty. Allied had also purchased Maker's Mark from the Samuels family of Louisville. The Samuels continued to run the business and had thrived under Allied's ownership. Tony explained to me what able shepherds they had been for other businesses like DCA, Tetley Tea, and Baskin-Robbins, which they had owned for decades.

Hales and Martin flew back to London that night, but before he left, Hales told me he was going to propose the purchase to his board. He assured me financing was no problem, that Allied had access to more than enough cash to do the deal. He was unequivocal when he told me, "Don't worry, we are going to buy the company."

It all happened over just four short hours, but probably four of the most important hours in our history. I was over the moon. I felt we had, at long last, found the right strategic buyer for our brand, and I believed the company and our franchise owners would be safe with Hales and Allied-Lyons. Exhausted, elated, and relieved, I enjoyed the first restful sleep in seven months. Victory might have come at one minute to midnight, but I was confident the company was indeed saved from disaster and that its best days lay ahead.

Hales quickly sent a team under the direction of John Garner, his finance chief, to go through our data room and confirm the numbers. We petitioned the court to push the auction date from Friday,

November 10, to Tuesday, November 14, informing the court that we had found a bidder who required another few days to get their bid in order. The court acceded to our request. The auction took place the morning of the fourteenth, after the Veterans Day holiday, and was held by phone. On the line was a representative of the court, Knightsbridge's representative Earl Rotman, me, our lawyers, Tony Hales, and Peter Solomon.

The bidding began with Knightsbridge repeating their existing offer of $43 per share. Hales quickly countered at $45.25 per share. I literally held my breath, but there was no response from Knights-bridge. It seemed like an eternity before the court representative declared the auction over and Allied-Lyons the winner. The total purchase price for all the shares came to $325 million, while the date for all shares to be tendered and the ownership changed over was January 1, 1990. And so began a new decade and new chapter in our story.

Dunkin' Donuts was one, if not the last, company to be attacked in the last gasps of the hostile takeover boom of the 1980s. Abuses abounded in those "greed is good," go-go days that finally caught up with many of the major players. Dennis Levine of Drexel was guilty of dealing in inside information with respect to takeover tar-gets, which led to the imprisonment of even bigger fish like preda-tor Ivan Boesky. Drexel Lambert went down; Michael Milken went straight to prison. Not long after, I learned of Unicorp's collapse.

The troubles began for our own predator, George Mann, in 1990 with the savings and loan crisis. He lost nearly $100 million from his failed Lincoln Savings. Soon, Unicorp was forced to sell Union Gas, its largest asset, reducing it to a shell of its former self. Mann was forced into retirement in 1990. I shudder to think what would have become of Dunkin' Donuts had he prevailed.

LESSON NINE:
Innovate-Test-Iterate

The world is constantly changing, and if an enterprise doesn't change with the times, it will perish. We had a mindset and processes that encouraged change as a way of life. We were constantly watching our competitors and others in our industry. We listened carefully to members of our own staff, our customers, and our franchise owners, and we were willing to change. We constantly tested many promising new ideas. Those that showed promise, we rolled out quickly; those that showed little or no promise, we shelved. We prided ourselves on our adaptability. Although most initiatives were developed in house, we had no shame in borrowing an idea from others and implementing it in our own way. The changes in purchasing and marketing in the late 1970s, as well as the innovations in store design and broadened distribution developed in the 1980s, all highlight our process of innovate-test-iterate in this era.

Yes, there were times we had to admit failure with one innovation or another and just walk away. Initiatives like our fish and chips chain, a donut factory in Delaware to manufacture frozen donuts to compete with Morton's frozen donuts, and our investment in a "fully automated" donut machine were just a few of our missteps. But we learned. Our modus operandi became "be nimble with our decisions." First, jump in early but don't bet the whole company. Second, if the gambit works, move to iterate. If it didn't, resist arrogance and stubbornness, admit failure, then close the whole thing down— and fast.

There's a lot of pressure in business to avoid risk, but one of the hallmarks of good executives is their willingness to make decisions. No one bats 1.000, not even Ted Williams, whose best year was .406. The trick is to edge out, don't bet the ranch until you're sure, and don't hesitate to pull the plug if things don't turn out as hoped. CEOs maintain the trust of their board and their team by consistently achieving promised annual objectives and, most importantly, ensuring the survivability of the business.

LESSON TEN:
Alignment Is Critical

As a result of my failure to convince my board of the efficacy of the Mister Donut acquisition in the fall of 1989, I learned an important lesson: never go into an important meeting, one where there will be a vote, without getting a vote count beforehand. My board had always voted with me in the past and I expected the same in this instance. That was to prove a bad assumption. Fear of being sued was the concern of a few and tipped the vote. Had I spoken to each of the board members before the meeting and teased out their concerns, we might have come to a different conclusion.

Only Art Fleisher, the partner from the firm Fried Frank— retained solely for the takeover—supported my proposal. Art, one of the most respected takeover lawyers in the country, thought the benefits outweighed the risks. Had I known of these issues before the meeting, I might have had Art reassure the directors and allay their fears regarding the Mr. Donut acquisition. But I neglected this important spade work beforehand and fear carried the day.

ERA 6: 1990–98

TEA AND CRUMPETS, ANYONE?

BACKGROUND

Tea and crumpets, anyone?

January 1, 1990, began a new decade for Dunkin' Donuts and me, as well as a brand-new chapter in our lives. As I reflect, the changes were not so noticeable or impactful for the business and our franchisees. I can't say the same for myself.

That first week, as control passed from our US stockholders to our new English owner, Allied-Lyons, I found myself headed to London for a meeting with more than one hundred UK financial analysts, each of them anxious to find out more about this donut company that was now part of their elite FTSE (Footsie 100).[1] I was also to make the rounds and meet the key executives of both Allied Breweries and J. Lyons Food Company.

George Bernard Shaw is credited with the quote "The British and the Americans are two great people divided by a common language." I found the differences, however, went far beyond language. I was to learn that class structure, social etiquette, and customs are also miles—or kilometers—apart. My first experiences that week in London were a harbinger of these differences.

The first day took me to both the Allied and Lyons headquarters where I was struck by the way they referred to their home offices. Allied was headquartered in downtown London at Allied House and J. Lyons was located on Hammersmith Road, ensconced in Cadby Hall. Giving a name to a headquarters building was definitely not an American tradition.

I was scheduled to meet our chairman that day. Not only had I never met anyone who had been knighted before, but he also had a very British, hyphenated name: Sir Derrick Holden-Brown. And so I faced a cultural dilemma. How to address him? Was it Derrick? Sir

Derrick? Or possibly Sir Brown or Sir Holden-Brown?? I ultimately chickened out and just said, "Very nice to meet you." At that moment, Alice in Wonderland came to mind; there was no doubt that I was in a very different world than the one I had inhabited over the past twenty-six years.

Both Allied Breweries and J. Lyons had long and storied histories of friendly mergers and acquisitions over a two-hundred-year history. First, as Allied Brewers, rolling up regional beer brewers since the eighteenth century, then merging with J. Lyons who had a similar history of rolling up food brands since the nineteenth century, and finally buying a number of spirits brands that had been formed in the twentieth century.

When Dunkin' Donuts joined the Allied-Lyons family, the firm was organized into three separate divisions: Allied Vintners, which was focused on wine and spirits worldwide; Allied Breweries, which operated more than three thousand pubs and one thousand Victoria Wine shops; and the food division headed by Tony Hales. It comprised the J. Lyons bakery and food production operations, DCA (Donut Corporation of America), Tetley Tea, and Baskin-Robbins. We were to be part of the food division. Each division had its own board and, in 1991, a year after we joined the group, I was elected to the food board.

ORGANIZATION

In this final chapter, I will be departing from the order I've used to describe each of the other five eras of my history with the company. In each of the other eras, I have told the story through the four functions I believe essential for an effective CEO, leading with a description of the strategy employed in that era. It is my belief that the decision about what a company wants to be, what objectives it must achieve (financial goals), and the five or so key levers you plan to focus on to achieve the mission and objectives are the most important senior management tasks in determining the future of an enterprise. In this last nine-year era of my leadership, however, organizational issues within my own business and within my parent company, Allied-Lyons, were to shape events and outcomes as much as, if not more than, the strategic issues we faced.

During the previous year, 1989, Tom Schwarz, Larry Hantman, and I were so busy trying to save the company from falling into the hands of George Mann that we spent no time thinking about how our world would change under new ownership—even relatively benign ownership. But change came and it came quickly.

Since we were no longer an independent public company, governance would move to the Allied-Lyons board in England. We would no longer have our own board of directors. As a result, we lost the counsel of our two longest-serving outside directors, Milt Brown, Lincoln Filene Professor of Retailing at the Harvard Business School, and Archie Southgate, managing partner of the Boston law firm Ropes & Gray. Both had provided meaningful strategic advice over the previous twenty years at critical junctures in our corporate life. I would certainly miss them.

We had other significant loss of talent as well. As a very effective senior management team with the top ten managers serving together for fifteen years, we had been able to punch way above our weight by attracting and retaining exceptional talent—partly through the generous use of stock options.

Allied-Lyons' compensation plan tied long-term compensation to the performance not of Dunkin' Donuts but to the stock price of Allied-Lyons. Further, the amount of stock available to my staff would be minimal, if any. It was an entirely new game. In short order, some of my top staff retired, while others left for jobs elsewhere. Tom Schwarz, our COO, left to become CEO of a large building supply chain. Sid Feltenstein, chief marketing officer, took a similar job at Burger King. Len Geller, head of international operations, left to do independent consulting. Rick Power, head of human resources, retired, as did my assistant of twenty-seven years, Lee Schultz. Since all cash management, borrowings, and stockholder relations would move to the parent company in London, the role of Dick Hart, treasurer, was made redundant. And most sadly, Ralph Gabellieri, head of store operations, was diagnosed with a terminal illness and wished to reduce some of his management responsibilities.

Fortunately, we had great bench strength. I was able to fill all the jobs except one from among existing executives. For that vacant position, leader of our international operations, I recruited a Brit who headed Allied's transition team.

After the acquisition, Allied sent a team to learn more about us and to help us transition into the Allied-Lyons family. The head of that team, Peter Harwood, had previously run one of Allied's regional pub companies. Although he didn't have any international experience, we got on well. And most importantly, I believed it essential we have someone from Allied as a member of my team who could teach us the ropes concerning how things worked in this new culture we were about to enter.

I was thoroughly committed to making this new marriage work and ensuring that the company we had all worked so hard to build over the last twenty-five years would continue to thrive. I felt it essential for us to continue to grow the system and earnings at our recent high level and avoid any major missteps. To do that, I would have to meld together a brand-new team and do it quickly—a particularly daunting task as it had to happen in real time as we faced a new owner from a different country with a very different culture.

A significant help in this era was the available female talent I could add to the senior executive team. Women played a very large role in the success of our business. It began with my mother's role in the launch of our industrial food service business, to Edna Demery's innovation of Munchkins®, to the board wives of the Philippine franchisees who revolutionized our distribution system by taking our products beyond the four walls of our store. Yet I am mindful that women didn't appear in the ranks of our senior management during much of my tenure.

The majority of my thirty-five-year CEO journey was from the 1960s through the 1980s. The culture with respect to women in the workplace was characterized by the TV series *Mad Men*. It seems true, as with most things, that the culture shaped us rather than the other way around. My aha moment occurred in the late 1980s while reading John Sculley's autobiography, *Odyssey*.[2] Sculley was then CEO of Apple. In his book, Sculley pointed out the great benefits that would accrue to society when it fully tapped the executive potential of women. As America awoke to the benefits, so did I. In my last era, the 1990s, two of the six executives who reported to me were women: our CFO and the head of human resources. I was also fortunate to have a longtime Dunkin' staffer Rosemary Elliott as my administrative assistant.

BRITISH MUSICAL CHAIRS

After twenty-seven years of being a CEO of a stand-alone company, I was now one of about twenty managing directors in a large, diversified, international corporation. I was responsible for about 5 percent of the group's trading profits. At Dunkin', the majority of my time had been spent helping my organization respond to ever-changing consumers and competition. In this new environment, however, I had to add an entirely new and very time-consuming dimension to my job: managing up!

During the last nine years of my stewardship, I was to have four different bosses. This proved to be a significant challenge, as each came to his task with his own unique business experience, competence, and style. I was compatible with some; with others, not so much. But in all cases, a good deal of my time—possibly the majority—would be spent educating, managing, and communicating upward. Gone were my directorships in the National Restaurant and International Franchise associations. In fact, most of my meetings where I kept in touch with trends and competitors were replaced with nine visits a year, of three or four days each, to headquarters in London. In addition, I had to be on call for three or four visits of similar length by officers from the UK visiting us.

My relationships in Allied-Lyons were almost exclusively in the retail and food divisions. I had minimal contact with the spirits arm of the company.

I found my new teammates welcoming and generally supportive, but I also observed some very real limitations to our fit within the group. I observed them as being very insular: all the members of the board and all senior and most company managing directors were

British. They had a very Anglo point of view. As case in point, they would hold their annual management meeting every year in London on the Fourth of July. Their backgrounds and key competences were in accounting, finance, and operations. Sir Derrick, our chairman, was himself a chartered accountant. Richard Martin, our CEO, was a brewer by trade. These talents were manifested by their historic success in pulling off complicated mergers and their ability to rationalize operations and continually take costs out of the business.

I found, with rare exceptions, they were seriously lacking in strategy and marketing know-how, the very areas I felt were my strengths. To the best of my knowledge, there wasn't a chief marketing officer in any of the retail or food operating companies except mine. The second most powerful executive after the managing director in each of the three main operating divisions was the finance director.

Tony Hales, my boss in that first year within the group, stood in stark contrast to the other executives I had met. He and I hit it off very well. In fact, because of his approach, I came to view him more as a partner than a boss. We were very much in tune on almost every issue. He was fascinated by our approach to focused geographical development, advertising, and brand building. While back in London, he paved the way to our getting home office support for our capital needs.

Tony enjoyed a meteoric rise in the Allied-Lyons group. At age thirty-eight, he went from managing director of a regional pub company to heading the Allied-Lyons food division. I found him to be great with people. He had a very light touch in dealing with us. He once told me that when entering the US he had been queried by the customs agent as to why he was visiting Dunkin' Donuts headquarters. Rather than claiming to represent the owners, he merely responded, "Just an investor." To me this response reflected the tone of our relationship. There was nothing dictatorial or directive in his manner. Unfortunately, after eighteen months, all that came to a crashing halt. Problems at headquarters in London caused major changes, among them our reporting relationships.

In March of 1991, Allied-Lyons reported that it had lost $285 million in the currency market. Cliff Hatch, who had become chief

financial officer after his family interests in Hiram Walker were purchased by Allied, resigned immediately. The company said that "it
is now evident that Allied-Lyons treasury was dealing in foreign currency instruments which were inappropriate and excessive, and, in
which it lacked the requisite trading skills." On May 4, 1991, an Associated Press news story reported that "Sir Derrick Holden-Brown,
68, in a letter to shareholders, plans to resign at the group's annual
meeting on July 4. Richard Martin, 58, will also resign and hand his
CEO post over in July to Anthony J Hales, 42." And with that, our
eighteen-month honeymoon ended.

I was to find Hales's ascension to group CEO a mixed blessing. I
was now to have a friend and collaborator in the highest operating
job in the company. My guess was Hales's proposal to buy us was his
biggest and boldest move in his short stay as head of J. Lyons. And
our subsequent performance, meeting and exceeding every projection in the eighteen months since we joined, had to be helpful in
the board's decision to elevate Tony to the top job. Unfortunately,
Hales's replacement was to prove a disaster.

David Jarvis, an international managing director from the spirits
division, was selected as Hales's replacement. Jarvis was the opposite
of Hales in every way: he was gruff, humorless, and imperious. He
rarely visited us. If there were matters to discuss, we would have to
visit him in London. He didn't seem particularly interested in learning about our business and how it differed from his experience in the
spirits business. Yet he was intent on showing us—me in particular—
exactly who was in charge. I remember one moment vividly, when
Jarvis, in an attempt to settle a disagreement between us, growled, "If
you're so damn smart how did you let your company get sold out from
under you?" This was not a marriage made in heaven. Fortunately, in
less than a year, major changes were afoot again at headquarters.

The Allied board had decided to strengthen its relationship with
the Pedro Domecq company of Spain, having purchased a 30 percent stake in Domecq when they acquired Hiram Walker in 1988.
Domecq was a key player in both Mexico and Europe, with leading
brands such as Sauza Tequila and Don Pedro and Fundador bran-
dies. Members of the Domecq family, the controlling shareholders,

complained in the press that they were dissatisfied with recent performance and their dividends. The Allied board decided the time might be right to purchase the remaining 70 percent, and David Jarvis was the right man to work on the project.

What I didn't know was that the board had also decided to exit the food business. They intended to close down that division entirely and sell all of the assets save two—ours and Baskin-Robbins—to raise the $800 million needed to purchase the shares of Domecq they didn't already own. As the most valuable jewel in that division, I was to learn we were being moved to the pub division, soon to be known as Allied Retailing.

I was getting a real education on life and politics in a large, diversified multinational company. I was also getting my third new boss in as many years. Fortunately, I don't believe any of our franchise owners or staff members, except for members of our operating committee, were aware of any of this tumult. The only visible change for our system occurred when the name of their parent company changed in 1994 from Allied-Lyons to Allied Domecq.

J. A. "Tony" Trigg, my new boss, was also a chartered accountant. He was formerly group controller but had been moved from the finance department to managing director of the pub estate after the currency scandal of 1991. I am guessing the board felt they had to clean house after the $285 million write-down. Since Trigg was blameless and had shown management promise, they wanted to find a useful place for him. Trigg was also a world-class rugby referee, often officiating at World Cup matches.

I found Trigg to be hardworking, precise, and direct, but inflexible. Once he had a cause or point of view, he would ceaselessly push it. In my opinion, neither his personality nor his training as an accountant or referee suited him to the task of heading an international retailing organization. A hard man not known for charm or tact, once he made up his mind, he'd pursue it to the end, irrespective of the feelings or input of others. Matters to him were black or white, like rugby rules. There wasn't a lot of gray in Trigg's world.

Trigg wanted to Anglicize Dunkin' Donuts by bringing this strange, to him, American operation increasingly under the control of its English owners. He insisted I retain a finance director from one of the regional UK pub companies. I demurred. His next approach was more appealing. At dinner one night in Boston, he floated an idea, asking: "Would you consider relinquishing your international operations in exchange for heading up a unified retailing company here in the United States including Baskin-Robbins? You haven't pushed international operations as much as we'd like and we can give it more emphasis from London." I asked for some time to think about his proposal. I wanted to talk to my team about the idea.

Months earlier, I had visited a franchisee in New York touting their success in colocating our Dunkin' stores with Pizza Hut and Kentucky Fried Chicken outlets in the city. It was an interesting idea. Colocating Baskin stores with Dunkin' seemed like a way to grow the flagging Baskin-Robbins business in the United States.

Trigg was right in that I hadn't been pushing international development full steam ahead at Dunkin'. The truth was, our results were very mixed and we had yet to "crack the code" on how to best grow our brand around the world. I was primarily concerned about two issues. The first was based on my experience in Japan and the problems associated with entrusting control of our brand in a large country to a third-party licensee. The second, and possibly more difficult to solve, was coffee preferences. Coffee was our main beverage and amounted to as much as 60 percent of our sales, yet preferences varied dramatically from country to country. Without strong beverage sales, our concept had real trouble providing satisfactory returns to warrant scalability.

The reasoning in London was, given Starbucks' overseas success, *why can't you do the same?* No doubt, Starbucks was having great success internationally, but we saw ourselves as very different, particularly as it related to overseas development. Although I honestly believed our coffee, with its high-quality South and Central American beans, moderately roasted, freshly delivered, ground on premises, richly brewed, and served with fresh light cream, made for a "sweeter," more flavorful cup than Starbucks, their concept was unique. Starbucks customers viewed their shops in the tradition of an Old World coffeehouse, as a third place where they could hang out in addition to their home and workplace. Starbucks, with their macchiatos and lattes, was selling ambiance and a bit of status as much as coffee. As a result, I believed their coffee product might vary from what was a traditional coffee offering in a country and still be successful. We, by contrast, relied primarily on the quality and freshness of our brew and our convenience and value, not ambiance or status. That positioning worked fine for us in the US and Canada where we were selling an American-style coffee to Americans. But, I believed, it was a much harder lift in Asia, the Middle East, or Latin America, where customers might be used to a very different hot beverage.

With respect to control of the brand in an international setting, we had developed a new way to go to market that we were about to test by opening in Mexico. In a populous country with such great potential, rather than relinquish development to one licensee, we planned to use the same development plan Wendy's used in successfully competing against McDonald's and Burger King. Our approach was to place our own country manager in Mexico with a small team and have them identify a number of regional franchisees to join in growing distribution in the country. That way we would control the rate and pace of development as well as the ad spend in the market and not be hostage to one country licensee. The viability of this approach was yet to be tested.

My team and I met to do a deep dive on Baskin-Robbins to see if a merger made sense. Ironically, Tony Hales's backup plan was to have the Baskin team run Dunkin' Donuts in the event I left after the acquisition. I could understand his concern and need for a plan B. I had read that more than 80 percent of entrepreneurial CEOs depart after their company changes hands. After three years, it became clear to them that I would stay, and we were by far the more accomplished and seasoned team among the two.

Baskin-Robbins had been a food service trailblazer for decades. Known for its wonderful and unique ice cream flavors and fanciful names, the brand had grown to more than two thousand stores around the world by 1992. Due to its limited menu, unit volumes were on the low side as were unit-level returns, but they were sufficient to warrant continued expansion and dominance in the away-from-home ice cream industry.

By the mid-1980s, however, their world, at least in the United States, changed dramatically for the worse. Häagen-Dazs and Ben and Jerry's, with their premium quality and equally interesting varieties, emerged on the scene in full force after being purchased by powerhouse consumer marketers Nestle and Unilever, respectively.

These brands entered the premium ice cream business in a big way; almost overnight they dominated the business in the US, not by opening retail stores but rather by selling pints and quarts in thirty thousand supermarkets and seventy thousand convenience stores. At that time, their quality, convenience, and price per ounce were superior to Baskin's. As a result, gallons sold per Baskin store fell from a high of fifteen thousand in 1980 to around ten thousand by the time we were doing our analysis in 1993. Possibly because of a less developed supermarket and convenience store distribution system overseas, Baskin-Robbins international stores did not suffer from these changes nearly as much.

Despite these sobering facts, we thought we might be able to add value through co-branding: the introduction of a beverage program based on Baskin's great flavor capabilities, ice cream cakes, increased consumer advertising, and store remodels. Relinquishing Dunkin's international stores wasn't seen as a big sacrifice. Less than 10 percent of our twenty-two-hundred-store system was overseas, and those stores provided minimal contribution to our overall profitability.

Whether to merge was, nevertheless, a tight call. Pivotal to our decision was our uncertainty over whether Trigg's plan was a request or a fait accompli. If we rejected the idea, would his commitment to rationalize and take costs out have him seek out the Baskin team to assume US responsibility? Or worse, would he have the managing director of Ansell's, our pub estate in the Midlands, take control of the US retailing operation? I knew how he simmered when I rejected a UK finance director. I also knew he desired greater control over the business and was preoccupied with rationalizing costs. I just wasn't sure how far he'd be willing to go.

In March of 1993, we agreed to take over Baskin-Robbins's US operations—all fifteen hundred or so retail stores and five ice cream manufacturing plants. This decision forced us to reorganize in a significant way. I elevated Jack Shafer, head of development at Dunkin', to be Dunkin's chief operating officer, and promoted Glenn Bacheller, Dunkin's chief marketing officer, to be chief operating officer at Baskin. Glenn and his family moved to Los Angeles to head our office in Glendale. Glenn had successfully succeeded Sid Feltenstein, who had moved on to the chief marketing job at Burger King after our sale to Allied in 1990.

Jack, in what I considered an inspired choice, hired Will Kussell from Reebok to replace Glenn at Dunkin'. Will was to prove a significant and beneficial change agent at Dunkin' over the next decade. Glenn, for his part, quickly put together a first-class marketing organization at Baskin by hiring a marketing chief from Clorox, who in turn hired some very bright young marketing people to round out his organization.

In the category of "be careful what you wish for," my successor moved forward aggressively overseas. Headquartered in London and pushed, I would guess, by Trigg, he invested heavily in international ice cream operations. This new international managing director, formerly a chartered accountant and pub company finance director, had no fast-food, marketing, or franchise experience. Within four years of the change, the international division lost $10.9 million due to unwise and hasty overexpansion.

I was beginning to see other cracks in the Allied wall. Despite our continued strong performance, the group was experiencing earnings reversals in all businesses save ours. The Domecq acquisition was viewed as a big disappointment, crippled by currency and political crises in Mexico as well as a slowdown in spirits sales worldwide. The pub estate was also suffering. When I joined the retail board, it was clear that the pub business was undergoing major changes: disappearing was the corner pub with its Victorian décor, replaced by restaurant operations that led with distinctive food offerings and served alcoholic beverages not as a focus but as a complement. Beer drinking in the UK was following the pattern of the US, going from local barrooms to bottles of beer consumed at home and on the go. Management was aware of these changes but, unlike some of their more nimble competitors, was slow to respond. And when they did, their response was tepid.

By contrast, Whitbread, another major pub estate in the UK, learned the restaurant business from the US when they purchased the franchise rights for both Pizza Hut and Fridays. Whitbread's managing director was a regular participant in the annual CEO roundtables we held, and which I attended, for restaurant companies in the US with sales of $250 million or greater. Despite my warnings at retail board meetings and private entreaties about the need to hire restaurant professionals and/or buy franchise rights for US concepts, Trigg was unable to see a world beyond our brewery heritage.

I was unsure about what our future might be within Allied Domecq. We clearly didn't fit with their orientation or business type. We were neither a spirits company nor a pub operator. They were oriented toward accounting, we toward marketing. I worried we might be sold to either provide cash to bolster a faltering spirits or pub division, or to finance the acquisition of another brand that better fit the group.

I didn't want our future to be in hands other than our own. I had been an early investor in Bain Capital's second fund and had been greatly impressed by their performance. I had watched and was impressed by Mitt Romney's 1994 losing run against Ted Kennedy for the Senate. Romney was the managing partner of Bain Capital, a private equity company headquartered in Boston. Bob White, second in command, a managing partner, and one of Romney's closest friends, was my neighbor.

I called Bob to see if there might be interest in helping management buy Dunkin' from Allied. His response was enthusiastic and immediate: "We sure would; let me talk to Mitt and set up an appointment." So, on a very snowy February day in 1995, Jack Shafer, Will Kussell, and I trekked into Boston to meet with Mitt and the senior officials at Bain Capital. They were very familiar with Dunkin' Donuts, and when we laid out our record and our prospects, they immediately indicated a great deal of interest. They urged me to open discussions with Allied to see if they would entertain a sale. Unfortunately, Allied's response was equally quick and emphatic. They rejected the idea unequivocally. I concluded, although our fit was tenuous, that losing our sales and profits would jeopardize their standings as an FSTE 100 company, which was an unacceptable outcome for a very proud and status-conscious group.

If that was a bit of bad luck, our fortunes were about to change serendipitously for the better. In the late autumn of 1995, I received a phone call from Tony Hales. He said, "I'm going to be in New York City next week. How would you like to fly down next Wednesday and keep me company for dinner? You pick the restaurant."

We met for an early dinner in a small Upper East Side Italian restaurant; the place had yet to get busy. After drinks and some small talk, I noticed that he seemed weary. He shared that he was in the city to talk to shareholders and analysts at Goldman Sachs. I was a bit surprised and inquired why he was doing this, traveling across the ocean for what I thought was clearly a job for his chief financial officer. It must have been the transatlantic travel and his exhaustion, but uncharacteristically he began to share his frustrations. In referring to his CFO, he said, "Oh my God, he's constantly sailing his boat in Europe. He's as lazy as all get out. I can't count on him for anything." I had never known Tony to complain about anything. I was feeling sorry for my old friend and blurted out, "I think enough time has passed since the currency crisis. Have you ever considered putting Trigg in as CFO? He's ideally suited for that job. I know that Stephen Alexander is without portfolio since we sold Tetley Tea; he'd make a great managing director of the pub estate." I don't know where the idea came from. I hadn't ever thought about it before that moment. But knowing the players, as I did, I spontaneously offered it as a solution.

I liked and trusted Stephen Alexander. We had served together for nearly three years on the J. Lyons board. I always found his thinking and comments sound and constructive. He loved and knew rock 'n' roll music history better than anyone I knew. Stephen's father, Sir Alex Alexander, had been a board member of Imperial

Tobacco and chairman of J. Lyons for ten years, then deputy chairman of Allied-Lyons before becoming managing director of Lehman Brothers Europe from 1989–1992. I believed that I and others in the retail division could work constructively with Stephen.

Tony didn't say a word. We had coffee and talked shop before parting for the evening. But on the plane ride home the next morning, I had a premonition that my off-the-cuff remarks had found a home in Hales's head. When I arrived back in Boston, I rushed to share the details of our conversation with Jack Shafer, speculating that I believed Hales liked the idea. I have never talked to Tony about that conversation again, but it came as no surprise several weeks later when we received the news: Tony Trigg would move from managing director of Allied Retail to CFO while Stephen Alexander would assume Trigg's responsibilities at retail.

This change in leadership was transformative. Stephen Alexander was very similar in style and approach to Tony Hales. He knew and appreciated marketing and the difference it can play in a company's fortunes. We were once again on the same page with our owner in a trusting and collaborative relationship. After three hard and trying years, our organizational travails had finally come to an end.

STRATEGY

In addition to meeting our new owners in London, there were two extremely pressing strategic issues we faced in those first few months of 1990.

The first was the need to dispose of our fifteen Chili's restaurants. The laws in nearly every state in the US then prohibited a distiller of spirits to be both a producer as well as a retailer of alcoholic beverages. Once we were acquired by Allied, the state of Connecticut, where we had several restaurants, issued us an ultimatum: "Sell your restaurants within ninety days or we will cancel your liquor licenses." I feared it wouldn't be long before other New England states would follow suit. Twenty-five percent of our sales in these restaurants were beer, wine, or spirits. A loss of our license would be a mortal blow. We had to sell the business before it was

worthless. Unfortunately, the country was in the middle of a recession and there weren't a lot of buyers. The parent company, Brinker
Restaurants, viewed real estate in the Northeast as expensive. As a
result, they were not prepared to buy and grow our small chain, at
least at that moment. Fortunately, we found a private equity buyer,
specializing in small-sized businesses, who purchased the chain before our liquor licenses were pulled. I later noted the new buyer was
able to sell their forty-five restaurants to Brinker in 1998, eight years
later, for $90 million: more than ten times what they paid for the
business. Their good fortune indicated our initial decision to bring
Chili's to the Northeast was justified.

The second important and pressing strategic issue was our acquisition of Mister Donut. Although our board of directors prevented
us from completing the purchase in 1989, in the waning days of the
hostile takeover battle, we were still convinced of the wisdom of the
acquisition and wanted to proceed. Importantly, Tony Hales shared
our enthusiasm. I wanted to move quickly before International Multifoods turned to another buyer.

Early in February, just a month after we joined the group, we were
ready to make our bid. Tony had secured the Allied board's approval. Allied had just laid out $325 million to purchase our approx-
imately eighteen hundred stores and now were to add another 550
Mister Donut shops in the United States for a mere $28 million. We
viewed this as a real bargain. In one fell swoop, we were to purchase
our main US competitor and provide a huge return to both Mister
Donut franchisees and the company by rebranding the Mister stores
to the Dunkin' Donuts brand. Another huge advantage of the purchase would be the addition of another 20 percent to our advertising spend after we fully converted.

The acquisition was completed before the end of February. I felt
strongly that, as this was our first request to Allied, our reputation
was at stake. We had to successfully execute and achieve our promised numbers.

The plan was to barnstorm the country, meeting all the Mister
Donut franchise owners and lay out our plan to them. We felt the
proposition was so compelling we'd be met with enthusiasm. Unfor-

tunately, change can be difficult and threatening to some, irrespective of potential benefits.

I turned to our former head of operations, Ralph Gabellieri, who was now battling a serious illness. I asked him if he would like to become president of Mister Donut and if he felt he had the interest and energy for the daunting task of profitably running the chain over the next several years while simultaneously spearheading conversion. I thought this last point of shrinking the chain and his own responsibilities would be a tough psychological hurdle for most managers, but not for Ralph. I was delighted when he enthusiastically accepted my offer. He was the perfect candidate for this job. He loved being president of a division, thought the assignment fit his skills, and most importantly, thought the job might add years to his life.

Ralph had built his reputation on skill, hard work, getting results, knowledge of the business, and an ironclad reputation for being a straight shooter, a man of his word. He had sacrificed for the company previously by moving to Texas in the 1970s and solving our problems there. He was beloved by the Dunkin' Donuts franchise owners. They knew that if Ralph gave his word you could bank on it: a reputation for honesty I believed would quickly become known to the Mister Donut franchisees.

Ralph picked several of his former trusted lieutenants to join him at Mister Donut, and off we went on a fifteen-city barnstorming tour to meet, greet, and try to convince the Mister Donut franchisees of the wisdom of conversion. We were sure of the benefits of our plan. Prior conversions of Mister Donut shops to Dunkin' had resulted in sales increases of between 10 and 20 percent. Conversion to Dunkin' would entitle the Mister franchisees to join the Dunkin' cooperative buying system and immediately lower their food costs by more than 10 percent. And finally, once we joined hands, we would have an advertising budget of nearly $30 million a year, allowing for advertising and future sales increases that would add immeasurably to the resale value of their shops. We calculated that it could take an investment of between $25,000 to $50,000 to properly rebadge their shops. But given the benefits, we believed it would take no more than one or two years to pay back that investment from added profits. We were prepared to arrange and guarantee the loans that might be needed for remodeling.

It came as a shock when we were forced to stop our program just as it launched. A small group of about nine Mister Donut franchisees filed a suit in federal court in Philadelphia. Those franchisees were arguing that the merger of the two largest donut and coffee companies in the US was an unfair monopoly. They were petitioning the court to reverse the sale, sending me and my team back to the same court where we had battled twenty years before in our class action lawsuit. Once again, Larry Hantman, our general counsel, stewarded our defense. Our lawyers argued the relevant market was not coffee and donuts but the now $400 billion away-from-home food service industry. The judge took some time to reach his decision but in the end decided fully in our favor. And once again we were back on the road, evangelists to the faith of donut and coffee shop conversion.

Ralph and his team performed brilliantly. We soon learned that in the Northeast, where the Dunkin' brand was much stronger than the Mister brand, sales improved not by 10–20 percent but on average by over 40 percent. Prior to this project, there had never been a real-life laboratory to measure brand strength. Finally, observers could see and measure the strength of a brand in all its glory. Where the brands had equal strength, markets around Pittsburgh and central Pennsylvania, sales upon conversion met our initial expectations of between 10–20 percent improvement. Where Dunkin' had no presence, such as Toronto, and Mister had a handful of stores, early conversions showed sales decreased by 10 percent. Ninety-five percent of the Mister chain were located in regions that supported at least a 10–20 percent sales improvement. The majority of stores were in the Northeast where we enjoyed those mind-boggling sales increases. Still, conversion was slow and required an immense amount of hand holding and trust building. In the end, after three years, we had successfully converted more than 450 Mister shops. And our reputation in London was established as a management team that delivers or exceeds what it promises. Our returns on the $28 million investment were through the roof.

Unfortunately, there were about a hundred Mister Donut stores we could not convince. Some seemed more interested in skimming sales and not paying taxes than in building a successful business. Once they were part of the Dunkin' program, we'd be able to calculate their real sales from co-op purchases and they would have to pay their agreed royalty and government taxes. In the end, Ralph suggested we set these last hundred free in exchange for these franchisees paying us three years of royalty payments. After the three years they would have to take their Mister Donut sign down and become independent donut shops where they could skim to their hearts content. Importantly, Ralph lived to see all this completed. And an illness that initially was projected to take his life within three years took more than six.

During this last era of my career, our objectives remained the same. Our goals for the period were to grow company profits by 15 percent on average per year. We also wished to ensure our franchisees earned at least a 15 percent return on their investments. The strategic initiatives to accomplish this were:

1. Dramatically broaden distribution through new points of sale including Mister Donut conversions, colocation of outlets with Baskin, and accelerating new shop openings
2. Add new products to the menus of both chains to drive same-store sales up by at least 4–5 percent per year
3. Invest in accelerated media spending with new and impactful advertising to support same-store sales growth
4. Launch a remodel program to update both chains and provide franchise owners a strong return from the remodels
5. Improve store standards relating to quality, service, and cleanliness, from a current 75 percent score to 78 percent

One of the biggest transformations of this era arrived with the hiring of Will Kussel as chief marketing officer at Dunkin' Donuts.

Will came from Reebok, where he began by managing their basket-ball business. He ultimately became vice president of Fitness World-wide, which he built into a $1.5 billion a year business. As part of the hiring process, Jack Shafer, now chief operating officer at Dunkin, requested that Will visit twenty-five Dunkin' shops and write his observations. This was a good screening tool and a useful way to gain insight from fresh marketing eyes. In any event, Jack must have been impressed by what he read as he quickly hired Will. Once onboard, Will requested $250,000 to hire an outside firm to do what he called a positioning study on Dunkin'. When Jack discussed the authorization with me, my response was, "What is a positioning study?"

I thought we were pretty sophisticated marketers, availing ourselves of annual attitude and usage studies and all kinds of research on new products and advertising effectiveness. As a result of my previous poor experiences with the consulting firm Arthur D. Little, I was more than a bit skeptical about this so-called positioning study. Finally, Jack explained the huge impact of proper positioning on our consumer communications, our new-products program, and our entire organization, especially in regards to defining whether we were a donut shop or a bakery or a coffee shop. He said, "Will senses that we are not as crisp about this as we could be and I agree. He's new and he's good and we should support him on this."

So Will hired Rick Rakowski of New Product Ventures and off they went to study our consumers and our competition. They also analyzed the trends over the years in what we sold by each line item on our menu. Two months go by and the big presentation on their findings is scheduled for the boardroom. Drum roll, please. . . . Rakowski took the podium and said, "We have studied your business extensively, and we have a new positioning for you, and it is C plus 1 [=] 3."

My heart fell to my shoes. I said to myself, "I just spent $250,000 for C plus 1 [=] 3, OMG."

Luckily, I controlled myself as Rakowski proceeded to explain how we had too long been a bakery culture. He continued, "With your change in your service delivery system, moving from the question mark counter to paper cups and self-service and now broadened distribution, your business has changed dramatically. Donuts are now only 15 percent of your sales. Coffee is over 60 percent and in some markets as high as 65 percent. Your advertising still features Michael Vale as Fred the Baker. Your new-products program is not focused on creating new beverage offerings but on cookies, muffins, and croissants. Even your name on your sign—Dunkin' Donuts—is an impediment to who you really are: you are Dunkin' Coffee, not Dunkin' Donuts." He explained that if all our thinking came through the lens of coffee plus any bakery item, the result would be a three, not a two. C plus 1 [=] 3. The whole is greater than the sum of its parts.

"*Wow*," I said to myself, "that makes a lot of sense. Glad I kept my mouth shut."

And so it was, our entire marketing focus changed as we became clearer about our positioning. Michael Vale retired after seventeen years of representing us, winning three Clio Awards. His departure was handled with grace and fanfare appropriate to a good marketing company. Fred's retirement was marked by a full motorcade through downtown Boston and a memorable advertising campaign featuring just-retired Larry Bird giving Fred tips on how to handle retirement. We hired Hill Holiday in Boston as our new advertising agency, and our new ads now started with a beauty shot and comments on the quality of our coffee, matched with any one of our delicious bakery items. Hill Holiday was the agency we hired thirty years earlier, when they were first founded, to help us launch Munchkins®. They are also the agency that created the great campaign "America Runs on Dunkin'," a campaign built on the thinking behind C plus 1 [=] 3.

This new positioning and thinking quickly began to pay big dividends. At the time, Rhode Island was unique in their love of iced coffee. Hard to believe in today's world, where iced coffee and other iced caffeinated beverages abound, that before 1996, iced coffee was popular only in the Ocean State.

That is when we introduced iced coffee to the world—and our iced coffee was a lot more than just pouring our great coffee over ice. We developed a unique brewing system, adding extra ground coffee, which ensured our finished brew stood up to the added ice and met our high standards.

We tested iced coffee in 1995 and rolled it out in 1996. Same-store sales sizzled. Iced coffee sales grew from less than 1 percent to close to 10 percent by 2009. In our best coffee markets, such as New England and New York, iced coffee rose to as high as 15–20 percent of our sales in warm weather months. The marketing team also developed and introduced a whole slew of flavored beverages, including hazelnut and French vanilla in 1996.

We also had some big wins in the bakery category that matched our success in beverages. During that year, Will Kussell became concerned about the growth of bagel chains like Bruegger's, Noah's, and Einstein Bros. and did a very abbreviated test of our own fresh-baked bagels. He and Jack Shafer approached me early one morning and said, "We'd like you to get approval from London for $26 million. We need $6 million to induce Heinz's bakery division to order and install a specialty bagel line to supply our stores. And we need to guarantee two thousand Chandley Ovens made in the UK, each costing $10,000, for our stores to provide controlled moist heat to serve our bagels. We've only tested this in a handful of stores for six weeks but our results are very, very good. Look, these competitive chains are growing like wildfire and are a big potential threat. With our advertising clout, we can be in the market overnight and head them all off at the pass."

Given their record on beverages, I decided on the spot I would make the ask. As Jack left my office, I shouted, "Hey, Jack, what's plan B if the bagels don't sell?" His answer: "I bend over and kiss my behind goodbye."

Luckily, that wasn't necessary. The bagels were an instant hit. We were nationwide and on air within a year. We plowed tens of millions of ad dollars behind our bagel introduction. Bagels rivaled donut sales in our stores. Same-store sales shot up and we were able to preempt the other chains while they were still in their infancy.

Across the country in Glendale, California, Glenn Bacheller was experiencing similar victories at Baskin-Robbins. That first year, he and his marketing team developed a proprietary cold drink they called Cappuccino Blast. Glenn quickly uncovered a hidden gem at Baskin: their flavor department.

The team that had created such all-time favorites as Jamoca Almond Fudge and Pralines 'N Cream had gone dry for several years. That all changed when Tony Gioia, the recently appointed vice president of supply, breathed new life into the company's flavor capabilities. He dedicated a portion of our Burbank ice cream plant to a cold-brew process to distill coffee extract from the highest quality Arabica coffee beans. This was decades before cold-brew coffee arrived on the scene.

This new cold-brew coffee extract became the flavor basis for Cappuccino Blast and proved to be an unmitigated winner. This was the first time in its history that Baskin offered a beverage.

Cappuccino Blast was such a success that the folks at Dunkin' began to rely on the Baskin-Robbins flavor team to help them with new product introductions. The first of these was Coolatta, another coffee-flavored cold drink. It was introduced at Dunkin' in 1997 and was a huge success. It provided Dunkin' Donuts stores a popular and proprietary cold beverage in the heretofore quiet 3:00 p.m. to 5:00 p.m. snack period. Almost overnight, Coolatta became a $200 million business at retail for Dunkin' Donuts. That one product alone made the merger between Dunkin' and Baskin-Robbins a winning proposition.

We had not had a remodeling program since the mid-1980s. The chain was looking a bit tired. But to date, despite a number of design attempts, we were unable to find a remodel that would provide our franchise owners a strong enough rate of return on investment we considered necessary. In the past we found it best to remodel every seven to ten years. It did wonders for our customers and our staff as well. When we freshened the shops, we found our staff became motivated and standards rose. We were very frustrated we could not add this important option that had historically improved sales and profits. We were aware that some retail chains required franchisees to remodel every ten years irrespective of whether there was a satisfactory return. We refused to do that. We had long concluded that it was our responsibility, as stewards of the brand, to ensure a fair return before we asked our franchise owners to invest in anything, let alone something as major as a store remodel. We believed if you required franchise owners to invest time or money without a satisfactory return, you would ultimately lose your followership.

Luckily, we never gave up trying. A task force organized to design the store of the future, yet again, came up with the answer. This specialized group comprised company managers, franchise owners, time and motion executives from Coca-Cola, one of our suppliers, and a group of graduate students from nearby Babson College who took on our assignment as a school project.

In their time and motion studies, they uncovered a phenomena heretofore unknown to us. They observed that when four customers were in line waiting to be served, there was at least a 25 percent balk rate. In other words, whether the customer was driving by in a car and looking into the store or to the drive-through window, if there were more than four people ahead of them, at least one in four prospective customers would drive past the store. We now knew our gaiting variable was size of the line. We created additional lines with more registers and replaced menu signs and headphone equipment to speed drive-through lines. The result finally cracked the code on how to achieve a satisfactory return on a remodeling investment. The chain was about to get a very needed and beneficial face-lift.

Now we come to the ideas and initiatives that were not such clear-cut winners. Most notable was colocating two or more complementary brands in one location. The benefits, if one could successfully pull it off, were enormous. By placing a Dunkin' Donuts within a building that also housed a sandwich brand and a snack offering, occupancy costs that amount to as much as 10 percent of sales could be slashed. Theoretically, one could obtain better, or more costly, locations because costs would be split and volumes higher. Parking lots, store personnel, utilities that once were needed to service one brand like Dunkin' could be leveraged at no or little additional cost to accommodate a sandwich brand at lunch, when Dunkin' was not particularly busy, as well as an ice cream brand like Baskin-Robbins in the evening when both Dunkin' and the sandwich brand were most likely slow. Remember, Dunkin' did 60 percent of its sales between 6:00 a.m. and 11:00 a.m., but most were open twenty-four hours a day.

The concept of colocating appeared to be working in New York City where a franchisee was leveraging scores of prime locations with two or more complementary brands. Concerns did exist that standards in these locations were below par, but the hope was that this had more to do with the franchisee than with the complexity of two operations in one location and the resultant strain on retail staff. At the time, PepsiCo, which owned major food service brands like Pizza Hut, Kentucky Fried Chicken, and Taco Bell, was equally impressed by cobranding. In fact, the day I toured the franchisee's operations in New York City, Steve Reinemund, then CEO of Pizza Hut, joined us. Ultimately, Pepsi spun off the restaurant brands into what is now Yum Brands. Even though Reinemund stayed on with the drinks company to become CEO of Pepsi, Yum Brands sustained its commitment to multibranding.

We believed that to receive the full benefits of cobranding, we needed to pair our two concepts, Dunkin' and Baskin, with a luncheon offering. Lunch accounted for 50 percent of the food-away-from-home market. We evaluated nearly fifteen different regional sandwich chains until we found what we considered the best fit. In 1997, we purchased a fifty-store chain called Togos, headquartered and primarily located in California. Togos had an almost cult following on the West Coast. They had built their reputation on their unique high-quality sandwiches assembled in full display in front of the customer.

While we were searching for a luncheon partner, we began to test cobranding by retrofitting Baskin ice cream counters into Dunkin' Donuts shops. To test the concept, we recruited six Dunkin' Donuts franchisees in the greater Boston area to incorporate a Baskin-Robbins shop into their existing stores. Outside signage gave equal billing to both brands. The investment for equipment and alterations was approximately $125,000 per location. Six months after the conversions, we met with the owners. Our expectation was to generate about $250,000 a year in additional sales per remodeled store, about the average for a stand-alone Baskin shop, as well as to achieve a targeted return of 25 percent on their investment.

Unfortunately, sales were half of what we expected and return on investment was negligible. It seems there was a slippage in impact and resultant sales when brands shared space. The company compensated these early pioneers on a portion of their remodeling costs to ensure they earned a reasonable return on their investment.

It took a number of iterations, altering both space and menu to support the more likely $125,000 a year in additional sales from ice cream.

These new configurations proved more successful. This cobranded format, Dunkin' and Baskin, continues to be developed in certain locations in the United States where appropriate.

I retired before the first triple-branded stores such as Togos were introduced. By all accounts, they were moderately successful but not as transformational as we had hoped. Sharing many concepts under one roof, these cobranded shops proved more cumbersome and harder to operate than anticipated. In 2007, Dunkin' sold Togos to the private equity company Mainsail Partners. Yum Brands, after more than a dozen years of colocating their many brands under one roof, also reduced focus on that format as well.

On balance, our initiatives had provided a lot more hits than misses. Over this nine-year period, we executed our strategy and achieved our objectives as store counts, same-store sales, and franchise owner profitability kept rising. We were now the seventh largest food service brand in the country as measured by total sales. Allied Domecq Retailing US was now generating $120 million a year in trading profit.

FAREWELL

With our organizational issues settled in London and our strategy working well in the United States, corporate life returned to normal. I was blessed with two very sound executives running the day-to-day operations of Dunkin' Donuts and Baskin-Robbins. Both Jack Shafer at Dunkin' and Glenn Bacheller at Baskin were demonstrating their ability to effectively and profitably run their brands.

After five trying years of adjusting to three very different divisional leaders, we were now comfortably ensconced within Allied Domecq. They had firmly weighed in that we—at least for the foreseeable future—were not going to be put up for sale. I still believed we were not an ideal fit within the group and would eventually be sold, but I had no way to determine if that would be years or decades down the road.

I felt we had successfully navigated the difficult passage from a stand-alone public company to a productive division of a large, British-owned, international enterprise. We had accomplished this transition with our culture, values, and earnings momentum essentially intact. I believed we were safe and that my job would soon be over. Friends who had gone through similar transitions had advised me with words of wisdom along these lines: "You will know when it is time to move on. The urgency and sense of purpose will not be the same." As I came to those very conclusions, I knew the time was right for a change. My sixtieth birthday was two years off and I still had energy and desire for another act, but I also knew it had to take place elsewhere.

To prepare, I used a familiar tool to help me plan for this next stage in my life. I had long believed the process, language, and framework of strategy creation we had used in business would work as well for individuals wishing to chart their future.

As a result, I put in writing my own personal mission statement, the three critical financial objectives I wished to achieve, and the four strategic initiatives I would follow to achieve those objectives. My mission was to be balanced in my life, focusing on family, health, and personal growth. I set some personal balance sheet and annual earnings goals and identified what initiatives I could institute to achieve them.

I was drawn to doing things that were generative. I had long harbored the notion of teaching. I was fortunate to have an opportunity to lead a company from near inception to worldwide operations.

I had seen and experienced a great deal and believed business school students might benefit from my experiences. I also thought my trials and tribulations, as a board member, might benefit younger CEOs who faced similar issues. So my plan was set.

I approached my boss, Stephen Alexander, and shared my plan for transition, recommending Jack Shafer to assume my job. He asked for a little time to talk it over with Tony Hales. Within a few weeks he called me and said, "Tony and I understand your desire to move on. We support it but are not as yet comfortable with Jack as we'd like to be. We are willing to give you a three-year paycheck when you leave if you will give us two more years to get us comfortable." I was touched and thanked them for their very generous offer and happily accepted with one condition. I requested some latitude in exploring my new life by investigating board and teaching opportunities while I was helping Jack assume his responsibilities. Three years earlier, they had given me permission to serve on the board of another publicly owned food service company but drew the line at that one extracurricular activity. Thankfully, they accepted my condition, and the door was open to explore additional possibilities.

Not long thereafter, I was invited to serve on a committee at Babson College, in the Boston suburb of Wellesley, Massachusetts. My oldest son had recently attended their one-year MBA program and I had been impressed by their early and full-throated focus on entrepreneurship. After a stint as a committee member, I was asked to join the college's Board of Trustees. I jumped at the opportunity, hoping my association in governance would lead to an adjunct professorship in their graduate school. As it turned out, it wasn't all that easy. I was neither a PhD nor a trained academician—either of which the college preferred before allowing one to teach in front of a classroom. When I pushed the subject with the dean, I was politely offered a position as executive-in-residence but not as an adjunct professor.

Serendipitously, an old acquaintance, Steve Spinelli, then a professor in the graduate school who was being promoted to vice provost and director of the Arthur M. Blank Center for Entrepreneurship at Babson, was looking for the right person to take over his class. As fate would have it, about twenty-five years earlier, I had met Spinelli when his coach at Western Maryland College, Jim Hindman, requested an appointment to discuss a business opportunity. It seems I was the only one, among the ten he asked, who gave him an audience.

He came to the meeting with three of his football charges in tow, his fullback, Steve Spinelli, among them. They laid out their business opportunity, which they had tested in Maryland the year before. They wanted to know if franchising was a way to roll it out. I thought their concept, Jiffy Lube, to be very viable and surely scalable. Spinelli joined Hindman in building Jiffy Lube, eventually selling out and returning to school for his MBA from Babson and PhD from the University of London.

When I told Spinelli the difficulty I was having getting a teaching assignment, he responded, "It would only be fitting if I returned the favor and gave you a chance to teach my class: Entrepreneurism through Franchising." Spinelli auditioned me, giving me a chance to teach a case before he turned his course over to me. Babson used the Socratic approach to teaching through the case method. Fortunately, I was familiar with this form of teaching from my own days as a Harvard Business School graduate student. That is how I began my teaching career. Teaching proved to be challenging and rewarding, everything I had hoped it would be.

The next two years were spent being available to Jack, liaising with London, and teaching at Babson. Managing my time wasn't a problem, but coping with the change was difficult for me. Once I declared my departure, my role changed from leader to advisor. I believe there can only be one leader at a time, and once that perception shifted, power naturally shifts as well. I believe that is as it should be. That said, if I had to do it again, I would make the farewell a much shorter time period, say six months. My team was very sensitive and saw to it my goodbye was marked with all the fanfare imaginable, but once the torch is passed, I believe one should exit the stage with all due haste.

As the transition neared, I was pleased with the manner in which my career was summed up by the *Boston Globe.* Business writer Chris Reidy wrote in his June 18, 1998, piece:

"After 35 years on the job, Robert M. Rosenberg is doing what many say Michael Jordan should do—go out on top. In September, the 60-year-old Rosenberg's duties as president and chief executive of Randolph-based Dunkin' Donuts will be assumed by his chosen successor, a 26-year company veteran, Jack Shafer, 54, who now serves as chief operating officer.

"Presided over by Rosenberg, the three chains (Dunkin', Baskin, and Togos) have 6,500 US stores and $2.5 billion in US sales last year. In 1963, his first year as president, Dunkin' Donuts had sales of $10 million. . . . In those years he has overseen the redesign of Dunkin' Donuts three or four times.

"Recently, Dunkin' Donuts has distanced itself a bit from its doughnut heritage to emphasize coffee, which accounted for $720 million of the chain's projected $1.9 billion in sales this fiscal year. While Rosenberg took his company public in 1968 and wooed Allied as a white knight during the hostile takeover era, perhaps his greatest triumph has been adapting to new trends."

Reidy quotes Jack Shafer in the article: "We are on a roll, don't anticipate any radical course corrections."

I officially retired on July 15, 1998, exactly thirty-five years from the date I became the CEO. It was bittersweet. I was leaving the day-to-day contact with the staff and franchise owners I had worked with and loved. But I was content in the personal satisfaction and fulfillment I felt and the knowledge that the best days for our system lay ahead.

LESSON ELEVEN:
Pick and Groom a Successor

One of the hallmarks of a good leader is the ability to groom a successor. In a previous lesson I proposed that one of the key events in the annual board calendar was to review organizational depth and create a methodology for choosing a successor to the CEO. In almost every case, it is most advisable to find a CEO successor from within the organization, someone who knows the culture and the players, represents the values of the organization, and has demonstrated an ability to consistently achieve its objectives.

I believe it is very difficult and problematic to bring in a new leader from outside the organization. Yes, there is the rare case when a company is in trouble and current management does not have an answer, and it may take an outsider to turn things around. There have certainly been cases where there is no internal candidate and the end of a CEO's career is in sight, where it might make sense to bring someone on board a few years before retirement to prepare them. Judging by the actions of the boards of the S&P 250, the wisdom of hiring from the inside is clear. Of the eighty-one newly named CEOs at those companies from 2014 through 2016, sixty-two were "lifers" who'd spent most of their careers with the company. Another ten had been hired primarily as CEO candidates and served several years at the company before being appointed. So overall, during those years, 89 percent of the new leaders (seventy-two out of eighty-one) were insiders.[3]

LESSON TWELVE:
Some Transferable Lessons for a Life Well Lived

I believe the same planning process I have proposed for a company works equally as well in a personal setting, as one structures the transitions in one's own life. Most retiring executives today still have many productive years ahead of them. In fact, I am now through my "second act" and have embarked on a third. For this to work, however, I believe my focus has to be planned and intentional. Great results are unlikely to just materialize.

As a transition is anticipated, I propose one undertakes a written plan to define a personal mission (what you want *to be* over the next three to five years). One should also establish a set of objectives or financial goals—in essence, what you want *to have* quantitatively. Lastly, it's useful to decide on the four to six strategic levers you plan to pull to allocate the scarce resources of time and money to achieve your mission and objectives.

I believe one should strive in life for a sense of fulfillment and satisfaction and, in the process, a feeling of peace. For me, these goals are most often achieved in service to others. But whatever your goals might be, I believe that armed with this planning process you are much more likely to achieve your dreams.

POSTSCRIPT

A year after my retirement, 1999, Allied Domecq sold their thirty-six-hundred-pub estate. Dunkin' Donuts and Baskin-Robbins were the only businesses they maintained from their former retailing division. Six years later, July 2005, they sold the entire business to Pernod Ricard, a French spirits company, with backing from US-based Fortune Brands. Pernod immediately put Dunkin' and Baskin up for sale, and Bain Capital finally had its opportunity to buy Dunkin. In December 2005, Bain, in combination with Carlyle Group and Thomas Lee Partners sharing equally, purchased the business, now known as Dunkin' Brands, for $2.4 billion. In July 2011, Dunkin' Brands went public. After twenty-one years, the company was, once again, an independent stand-alone company, master of its destiny, to rise or fall based on its own merits.

As of this writing, February 2020, the public market value of Dunkin' Brands was $6.5 billion. A long journey from when the first shop opened in 1950 on the Southern Artery in Quincy, Massachusetts—testimony to the skill and ability of succeeding leaders to grow from the solid foundation we had built.

ADDENDUM

Wisdom can come in all forms, one of which could be from the written word. That was the case for me. Wisdom came from business books as well as novels. I can't overstate the impact *The Best and the*

Brightest, by David Halberstam, had on me. In fact, when I think about books that have helped me, I am often reminded of a saying my brother, Donald, frequently repeated: "When the student is ready, a teacher will appear." Many times, the "teacher" came in the form of a book I was reading.

For example, in reading *Studs Lonigan,* a novel by James Farrell about a young man growing up in early-twentieth-century Chicago, I came to understand that most every city has a "right side" and "wrong side" of the tracks. Beyond enjoying the story, it occurred to me that rather than running around the country visiting prospective sites in order to gauge their appropriateness for a store, my time might be better spent accessing more hard data about each city. Based on that insight, we began to use the demographic data and regression analysis to help us rank markets, map out selected cities, then prioritize locations within the city. In the end, this was a significantly smarter and more reliable way to pick new locations, in contrast to me standing at some prospective site, sniffing at the air and looking around for God knows what before declaring either a thumbs-up or thumbs-down.

Below is a list of books that have helped me over the years.

Chris Zook with James Allen, *Profit from the Core* (Harvard Business School Press, 2001). Substantiates value destruction when diversifying from a company's core business.

Chris Zook, *Beyond the Core* (Harvard Business School Press, 2004). Expand your market without abandoning your roots.

John Heider, *The Tao of Leadership* (Wildwood House Ltd-UK, 1986). Timeless lessons and advice on leadership.

Max DePree, *Leadership Is an Art* (Crown Publishing, 1989). Details that the responsibility of a leader is to define reality and to say "thank you."

Ram Charan, Dennis Carey, and Michael Useem, *Boards That Lead* (Harvard Business School Publishing, 2014). When a board should take charge. When to partner and when to stay out of the way.

Matthew Budd, MD, Larry Rothstein, *You Are What You Say*, chapter 4 only (Crown Publishing, 2000). The power and use of language.

David Halberstam, *The Best and the Brightest* (Random House, 1972). The dangers of hubris.

Rosabeth Moss Kanter, *The Change Masters* (Simon and Schuster, 1983). How to best encourage innovation and change in an organization.

Jim Collins, *Good to Great* (Harper and Row, 2001). What makes for an enduring company.

John Kotter, *Leading Change* (Harvard Business School Press, 1996). An action plan on how to best lead change in an organization.

Don Clifford Jr. and Dick Cavanagh, *The Winning Performance* (Bantam Books, 1985). How America's high-growth midsize companies succeed.

Peter Drucker, *Managing for the Future* (Penguin Books, 1992). A wide array of insights for managers in an ever-changing world.

Michael Eisner, *Working Together: Why Great Partnerships Succeed* (Harper Collins, 2010). Highly successful business collaborations.

Acknowledgments

As I reflect on my career, I believe every important project I have been associated with has been a team effort. That was truly the case in the creation of this book. I have a lot of people to thank for their help. I want to thank two women who were critical to the telling of this story. First and foremost, my life partner of twenty years, Mary Wolfson. Mary not only encouraged me to tell this story, but patiently discussed each chapter and edited each of many drafts. The other is Erica Ferencik. Erica is not only a friend, but a first-class author of several published novels. It was Erica who provided the idea for the title, as well as determined where in the text to best introduce the reader to the story. Erica, with her superior technical and literary skills, kept track of countless versions of the manuscript through every round of edits, providing essential coaching and advice.

I am also grateful to the many friends, family, and former colleagues who participated in refining different elements of the book. Former Dunkin' Donuts teammates Tom Schwarz, Sid Feltenstein, Larry Hantman, Len Geller, Jack Shafer, Will Kussell, Tony Gioia, Kim Lopdrup, Leonard Swartz, and Frank Tumminello graciously agreed to be interviewed and allowed me to tap their memories. I am also grateful to Peter Solomon for his review of the chapter in which he played such a pivotal role. Similarly, I owe a debt to Phil Zeidman, partner in the firm of DLA Piper, for his review and suggestions relating to the material on franchising.

Friends and family generously volunteered their time and advice. Some contributed their insights on portions of the tale, such as my sister Carol Silverstein and my daughter Jennifer; others served as beta readers providing important feedback. These were Barbara Alfond; Cliff Hudson; Sid Feltenstein; Tom Schwarz; Dr. Henry Friedman; Roberta Sydney; Will Osborne; my brother, Donald Rosenberg; my former sister-in-law, Terry Rosenberg; Lenard Zide; Richard Talkin; Jason Harlan; Jessica Sirmans; Riki Cobler; my sons, John Rosenberg and James Rosenberg; and Angela Santopinto.

Finally, I thank my agent, Esmond Harmsworth III, who believed the story of Dunkin' Donuts was a tale worth telling. Lastly, I'm grateful to my editor, Tim Burgard, and the entire team at HarperCollins for their unflagging support during each phase of the publishing process.

Notes

INTRODUCTION

1. See Dunkin' beats Starbucks.com. A&G research conducted double-blind tests among 476 coffee drinkers in ten large American cities, revealing a preference. The raw scores showed that 54 percent favored Dunkin', 39.3 percent preferred Starbucks, and 6.3 percent had no preference.

2. As of February 2020, Dunkin' Brands includes both Dunkin' and Baskin-Robbins.

ERA 1: 1963–68

1. In the early 1960s, Universal Food Systems consisted of eight separate businesses: 1) Industrial Luncheon Service, a 150-truck catering service, 2) approximately twenty industrial cafeterias, providing catering in-house for larger factories and offices, 3) Menu-Mat, a vending company serving industrial, office, and retail settings, 4) Howdy Beef n' Burger, a chain of fifteen McDonald's-like fast-food restaurants, 5) Dunkin' Donuts House of Pancakes, three large restaurants patented in style, similar to International House of Pancakes, 6) Willie's, a full-service deli in Providence, RI, 7) One hundred Dunkin' Donuts shops, and 8) a 50 percent interest in The Leaning Tower of Pizza, a drive-in pizza parlor selling pies to eat in and to take home.

2. Montgomery Ward was a once well-known and able competitor to Sears in both their catalogue and retail store businesses. But after World War II, the controlling stockholder and manager of Montgomery Ward, Sewell Avery, believed the world economy was fragile and in store for another potential depression. Avery contracted while Sears expanded in the 1950s. In the '60s, Montgomery Ward began a forty-year slide from relevance until its bankruptcy in 2000.

3. The traditional spelling was doughnuts. "Donuts" was chosen instead because it better balanced Dunkin' as a logo and in signage. Donuts

had fewer letters; therefore, it was a less expensive sign to build and easier to get sign permits under local ordinances.

4. In 1955, I matriculated to the Kellogg Center of Hotel and Restaurant Administration at Michigan State University. After my freshman year, I transferred to the School of Hotel and Restaurant Administration at Cornell University, from which I graduated in 1959.

5. One of my early salvos in the Donut War was to fulfill a commitment to my father to write a book that would right the omissions in Harry Kursh's *The Franchise Boom*. I wanted to tell the story of Dunkin' Donuts and my dad, the rightful originator of the new and growing donut and coffee shop industry. In 1968, McGraw-Hill published *Profits from Franchising*, a book I coauthored with Madelon Bedell, a former *Fortune* staffer. Our book intended to set the record straight. The battle of the books, however, was not the critical turning point in the Donut Wars. Rather, I believed these meaningful battles turned on differences in strategy and organization.

6. When I joined the company in 1963, I, with the agreement of my father, worked with Price Waterhouse, our accounting firm, to develop a gift-giving program that allowed my father to gift $3,000 a year to each family member. My father did not want to pay taxes on the gifts, and the amount was the allowable annual tax-free gift in those years. The stock split 17 for 1 on the eve of the offering. As a result, the $3,000-a-year gifts granted in 1963 and onward became quite valuable by public offering time.

7. Malcolm Gladwell, *Outliers: The Story of Success* (Boston: Little, Brown, 2008).

8. Catherine Schnaubelt, "Transitioning Your Business to the Next Generation," *Forbes*, August 17, 2018. Quotes Family Business Institute as source of 30 percent statistic.

9. Dairies found they could add substantial shelf life to their dairy products by subjecting them to periods of very high heat before packaging—thus they created a new category of ultra-pasteurization.

ERA 2: 1969–73

1. The law of large numbers here means the larger the base, the greater the growth required to maintain the same percentage.

2. Often referred to as a SWOT analysis.

ERA 3: 1974–80

1. Michael Eisner, *Working Together: Why Great Partnerships Succeed* (New York, HarperBusiness, 2010).

2. Donald K. Clifford and Richard E. Cavanagh, *The Winning Performance: How America's High-Growth Midsize Companies Succeed* (New York: Bantam, 1985), p. 137.

3. These fine colleagues were Larry Hantman, James Dangelo, Sidney J. Feldenstein Jr., Ralph Gabellieri, Len Geller, Bernie Patriacca, Rick Power, Dick Hart, and Tom Burger.

ERA 4: 1980–83

1. *Bakery Magazine*, August 1978.

2. *Bakery Magazine*, August 1978.

3. 1983 Dunkin' Donuts stockholder's annual report, p. 8.

4. Donald K. Clifford and Richard E. Cavanagh, *The Winning Performance*, p. 134.

5. Peter Lynch with John Rothchild, *One Up on Wall Street* (New York: Simon and Schuster, 1989), p. 81.

6. For my calculations, I include an owner's draw as an expense; however, I calculate that draw based on what a typical manager might be paid for that position.

ERA 5: 1983–90

1. Knowledge@Wharton, November 5, 2012.

2. The Securities and Exchange Commission requires anyone who accumulates more than 5 percent of a publicly traded stock to file a form 13D within ten days of when the purchase is or exceeds 5 percent. Often this filing indicates someone is interested in a change in control, which most often heightens the stock price of the targeted company.

ERA 6: 1990–98

1. The *Financial Times* listing of the UK's hundred largest companies by market capitalization, comparable to the US Dow Jones Index listing of thirty US companies.

2. John Sculley, *Odyssey* (New York: Harper and Row, 1987).

3. *Fortune* magazine, October 25, 2017, management.marc.feigen.ceos.

Index